# Fashion Sewing

# Fashion Sewing

Renée Robinson

Studio Vista
London

This book is dedicated to only he knows who and why, with thanks.

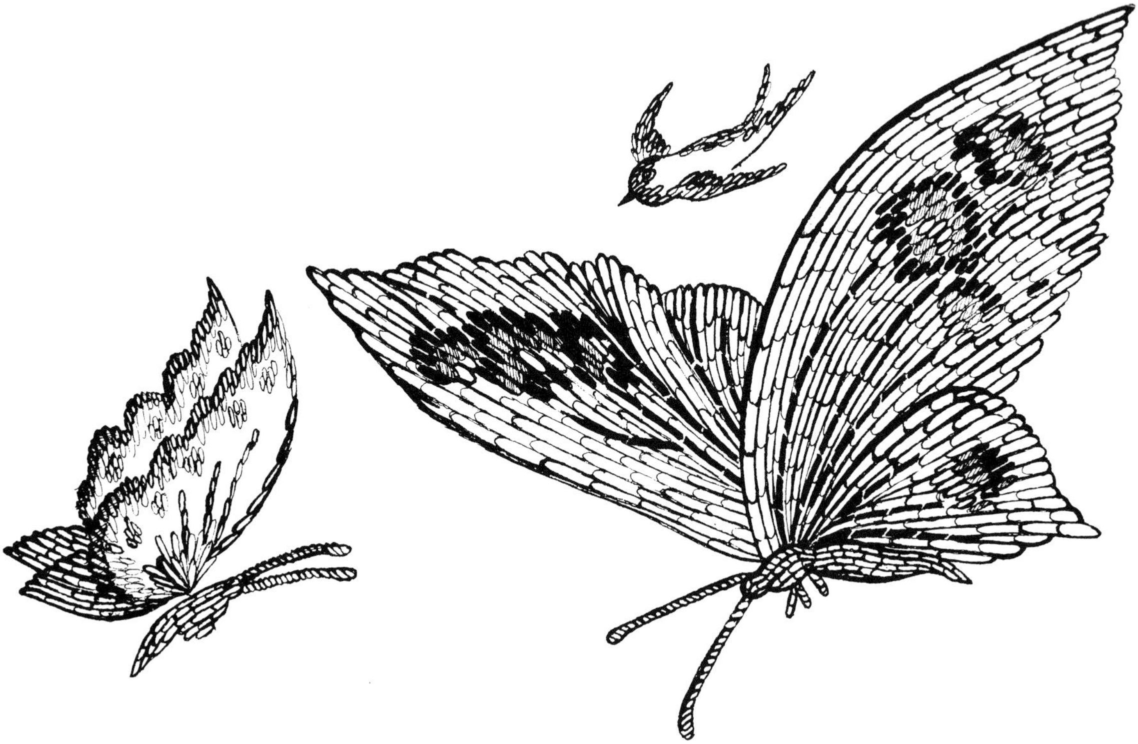

A Studio Vista book published by
Cassell & Collier Macmillan Publishers Ltd.,
35 Red Lion Square, London WC1R 4SG
and at Sydney, Auckland, Toronto, Johannesburg,
an affiliate of the Macmillan Publishing Co. Inc.,
New York


First published in Great Britain 1977


Set in 11/13 Garamond
Printed in Great Britain by Butler & Tanner Ltd., Frome and London

ISBN 0 289 70724 2

# Contents

# *Introduction*

Model clothes are instantly recognizable, often because of that hint of the exclusive afforded by hand sewn trimmings and decorations. They are also expensive, for hand finishing is always costly. But if you have the time and patience you can give your clothes that same couturier touch for next to nothing.

Whether you are a beginner or an experienced dressmaker, this book will help you introduce individuality and flair into your wardrobe, showing how to adapt and use to advantage all kinds of fashionable sewing techniques, many of them revived from the twenties and thirties.

This is a book of inspiration and ideas, with a new technique on every spread. Topics have been loosely grouped under general headings – trims, edgings, embroidery, and so on – for ease of comparison. Although it is assumed that you have some basic knowledge of sewing and embroidery, most of the techniques and stitches are explained in detail and accompanied by working diagrams. As you become more expert, you will want to turn to specialist volumes on such subjects as smocking and patchwork for an even wider range of stitches.

Use these ideas in conjunction with good commercial dress patterns, allowing instinct and imagination to guide your choice of fabric and colour. Allow a sixth sense to develop and soon you will have that magic touch that turns ordinary dressmaking into something original and exciting.

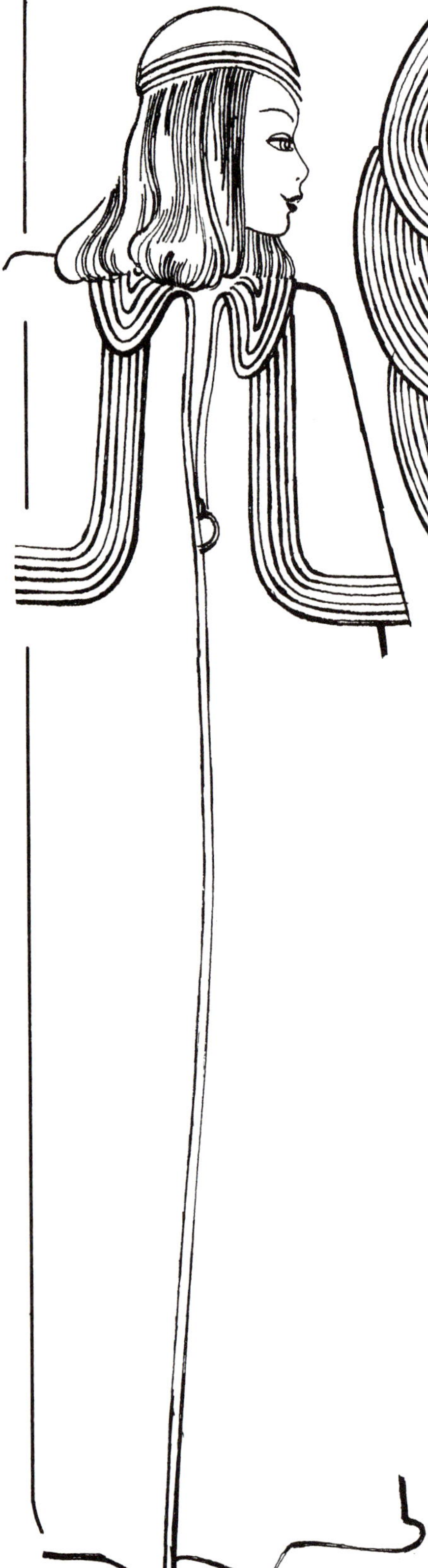

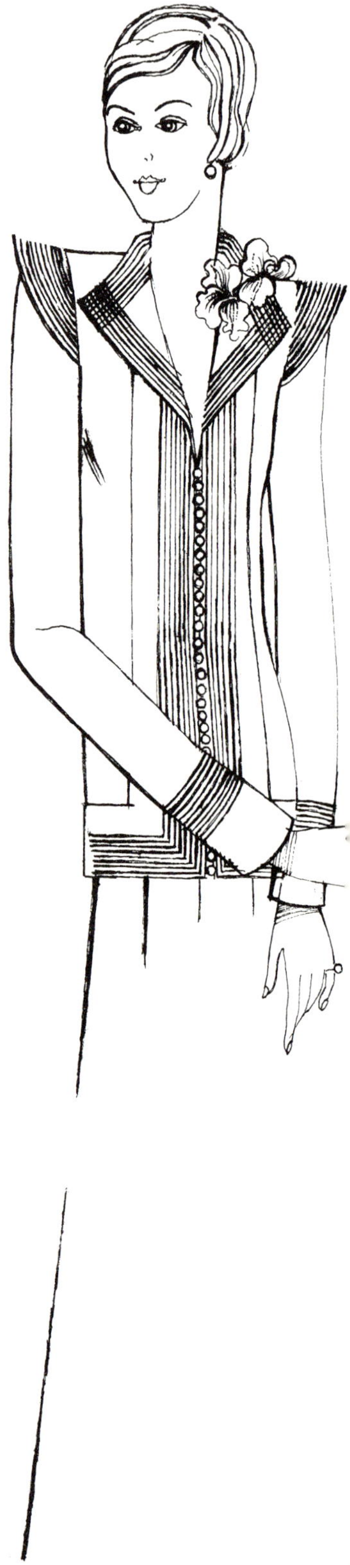

# *Topstitching*

Topstitch for that professional tailored look. Not only is it functional, holding seams and edges down flat, but it can be used for sporting, tailored or masculine looks.

You can vary the scale of the stitching according to the type of fabric and the style of the garment. On coatings distances of $\frac{3}{4}$–$1\frac{1}{2}$ in. (20–40 mm) between the stitching and seams or edges are not out of place; they create a heavy ridge between the stitching and the edge, making an important decorative feature. On flat or light cloth, use edge stitching or narrow stitching.

Stitching interest need not be confined to outlining edges, pockets and collars. Combine one, two, or three lines of stitching (b) or cross-hatching (c) to form geometric patterns with interesting textural effects. Use topstitching, too, as a decorative strengthener for heads of pleats, bound buttonholes and slit pocket ends. Try stitched arrow-heads, ovals, circles or rectangles. You can even use banks of diagonal stitching on corners of coat hems or on undercollars (a).

**Choosing the thread**

Use a contrasting colour or a heavy thread for emphasis. Buttonhole twist or dual reels of mercerized cotton can be threaded through a large-eyed machine needle especially suited to stitching on thick fabrics. Make zigzag topstitching with an electric machine; or run a cord through the zigzag for raised topstitching that looks good on flannels, denims and flat fabrics.

**Stitching**

In order to achieve good results, always check your tension and stitch size, and be sure the machine needle is sharp and of the correct size. Try out the stitching on a sample piece of fabric first. For straight, evenly spaced work, use a notched guide; or for close, narrow stitchery press the machine foot hard against the previous line of stitches to guide you. Some automatic machines have a metal guide (d). Always start and finish work with back stitches; see that your stitches do not drag; and remember that nothing is messier or uglier than crooked topstitching.

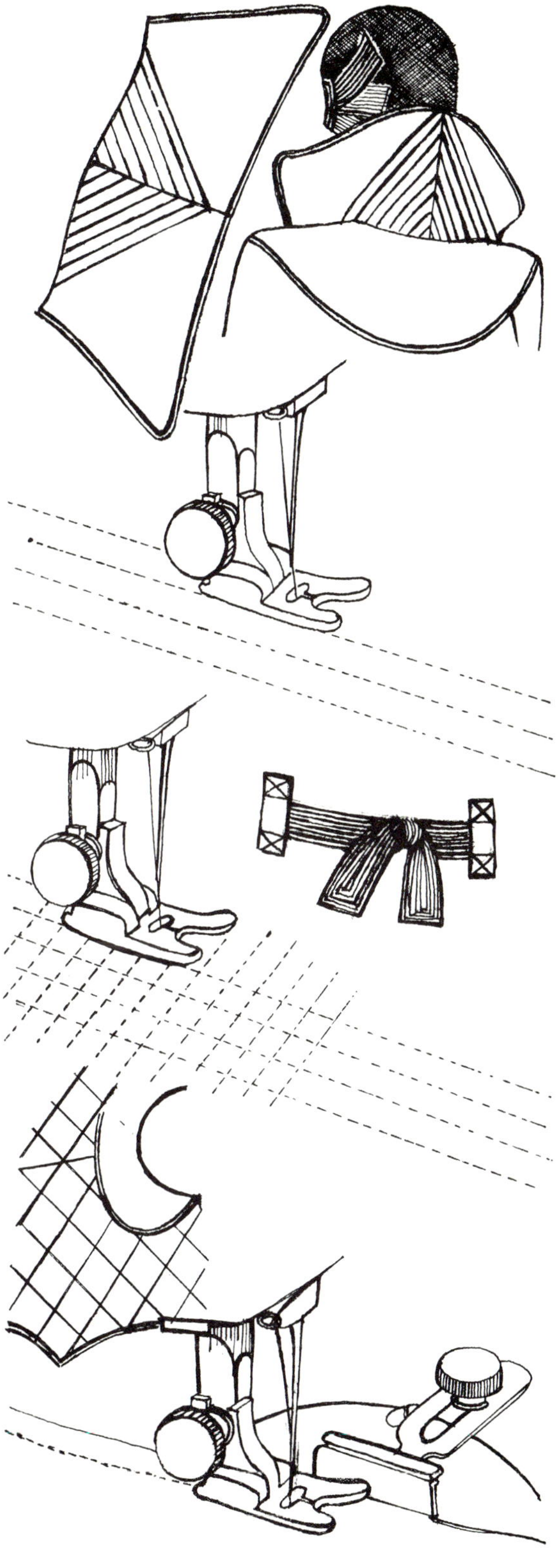

a

b

c

d

# *Tucking*

Tucking has a touch of tenderness about it. In recent years its popularity has increased, encouraged in part by films such as *The Great Gatsby, The Boy Friend* and *My Fair Lady*.

There are a million pretty uses for tucking on clothes, varying from pin-tucks to widely spaced broad tucks and even curved tucks. Groups of tucks can be worked in formal bands or in horizontal, vertical or crosswise sections, giving a geometric look to the design. Bands of formally arranged tucking look immaculate on a severe dress, but they can also look pretty on a romantic blouse, especially if the tucks are flanked by lace frills and embroidery. They can look sporting too, with a geometric interplay of tucks emphasizing the line or detail of a style or an interesting cut. And bands of vertical tucking bursting into pleats above the knee will make a 'swingy' dress look even more youthful.

**Cutting the fabric**

First decide on the widths and number of tucks required for your design. Allow twice the width of a tuck for each one, adding the extra to the sides of your pattern. Alternatively, if you will be making a great number of tucks, cut a large rectangle of fabric and make the tucks before laying the pattern section on it for cutting in the usual manner.

The tucks must be made along the exact grain of the fabric, the spacing being clearly marked with the aid of a notched guide (a).

**Pin-tucks**

These are the easiest tucks to make. First crease a fold along the grain where the tuck is to be. Then run or machine stitch $\frac{1}{8}$ in. (3 mm) from the fold. Mark the next tuck by using your tuck guide. Again, crease the fabric along the grain and stitch. Pin-tucks may be spaced evenly across your fabric or arranged in groups (b). Cross tucking can also be made by this method. First make all the vertical tucks and then cross them with horizontal ones, being careful to space them evenly (c).

**Wide tucks**

To ensure the even spacing of wider tucks, it is essential to mark the fabric. Decide first on the width and spacing which will best suit your purpose. For example, if you wish to make $\frac{1}{4}$ in. (6 mm) tucks 1 in. (25 mm) apart, prepare a notched guide as follows. Cut a narrow piece of card and make a notch 1 in. (25 mm) from the top. Make a second notch $\frac{1}{4}$ in. (6 mm) below it, and a third $\frac{1}{4}$ in. (6 mm) below that. Use the guide when marking the fabric. Crease the fabric along the centre mark and stitch $\frac{1}{4}$ in. (6 mm) from the folded edge. Graduated tucks should be marked and stitched in the same way, increasing or decreasing their widths or spacing as required. It is usual to place the widest tuck and spacing nearest the hem (e).

**Shell-edged tucking** (d)

This decorative finish is suitable for use on fine fabrics. Run stitch the tuck at regular intervals making a gathering stitch up and down and pulling it tight.

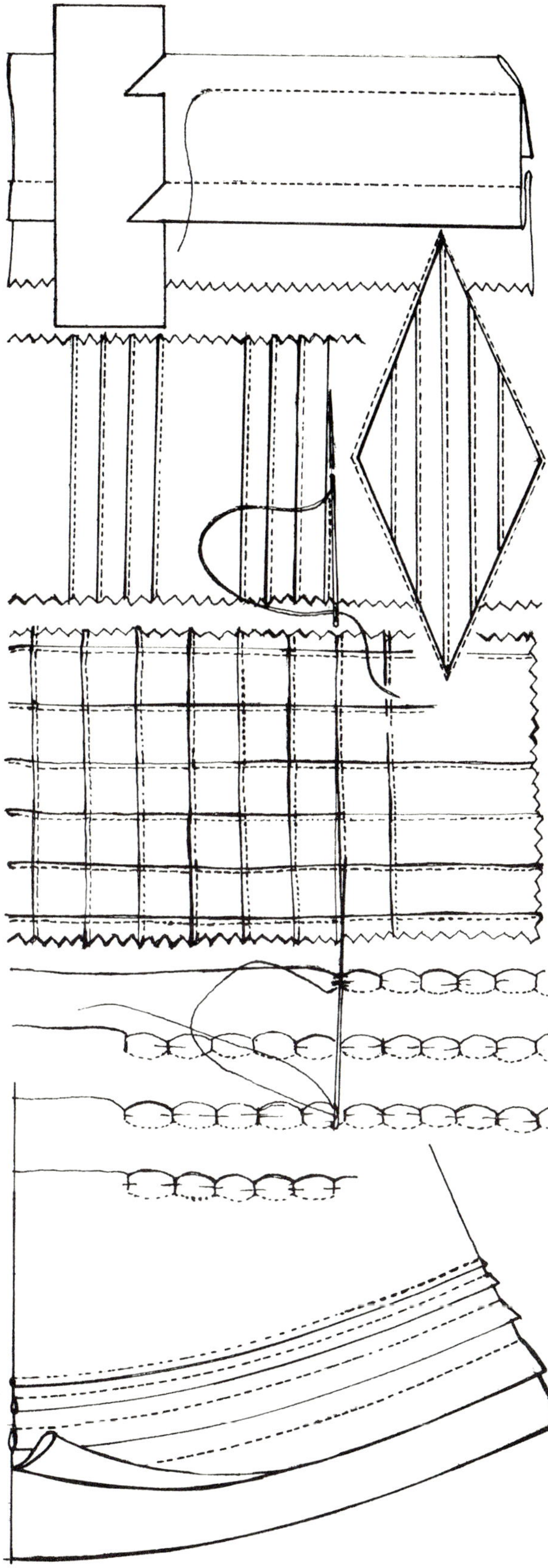

a

b

c

d

e

# *Drawn thread work*

Even if you have not attempted drawn thread work before, with nimble fingers, a little patience and a fair amount of concentration you will be able to achieve highly decorative ornamental patterns. Drawn thread work involves withdrawing parallel groups of warp or weft threads from the fabric and hem stitching the remaining loose threads to form vertical, zigzag or lacy patterns. The open corner sections are stitched with spider's web or flower detailing. The whole work can then be decorated with extra stitches interlacing the open patterns of threads.

For an even more decorative effect, work round the threadwork with feather stitching, satin stitched spots, chevrons and squares, French knots, open Cretan or scroll stitch. You may include wooden beads or sparkling sequins in your finished design.

Drawn thread work is most effective when used on simply cut garments, for complicated seam lines will interrupt the natural flow of the work. It is suitable for use on dresses, casual pants suits, beach pyjamas and tunics made in linen type fabrics. With a little more skill it may also be applied to fine cotton, lawn and even crêpe-de-chine. However, it would be best to make your first attempts on simple linen or coarsely woven cotton.

**First attempts**

Experiment on a small cutting of fabric, marking the section to be decorated, $\frac{1}{2}$ in. (12 mm) wide by 4 in. (100 mm) long, along the grain. Cut the horizontal threads $\frac{1}{2}$ in. (12 mm) inside the marks and lift out the threads between the cuts one by one with a pin. Now lift out the $\frac{1}{2}$ in. (12 mm) ends as far as the marks, and with a large-eyed needle weave each one back into the fabric so that the frayed ends do not show (a). Next, using a matching thread drawn from a long edge of the fabric, or matching sewing thread, work in hem stitch along the bottom line, arranging the threads in groups (b).

Start by bringing the needle up two threads below the right-hand corner of the open work. Next make a stitch behind two or more loose threads. Insert the needle behind the same loose threads, bringing it through the fabric two threads down and two threads along, as shown. Repeat this stitch until the bottom edge is complete. Work a similar group of hem stitches along the opposite edge (c). The 'open ladder' work can be interlaced or decorated as required (d). Alternatively, make a zigzag design by stitching the threads in groups of four and taking up two threads from each of two adjoining groups when stitching the second edge (e).

For your next experiment mark a 4 in. (100 mm) square on the exact grain of a piece of fabric. Mark a second square $\frac{1}{2}$ in. (12 mm) inside it. Work as before, cutting and lifting out the threads. You will find that you are left with a hole in each corner when you thread the ends back into the fabric. After hem stitching, fill in the corners with flower or spider's-web patterns (f).

Now you are ready to start work on a garment. If it is a coarsely woven fabric you may prefer to hem stitch in matching sewing thread, or even in a toning or contrasting shade.

a

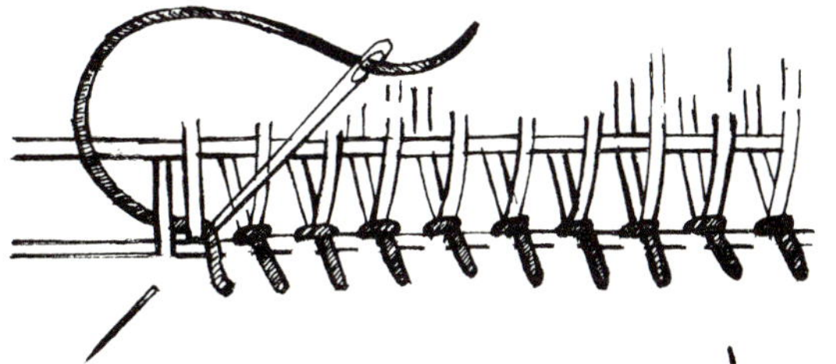
b

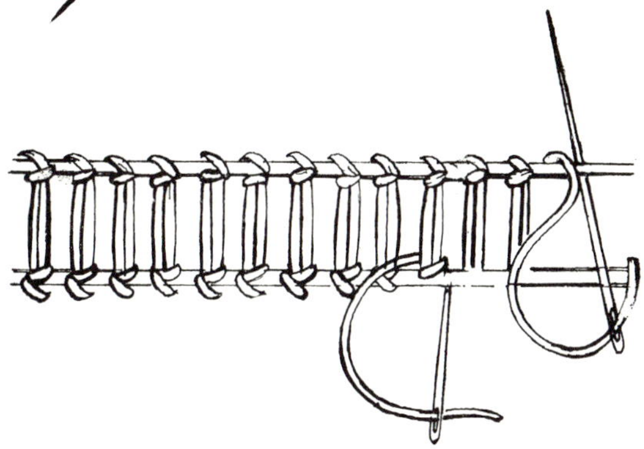
c

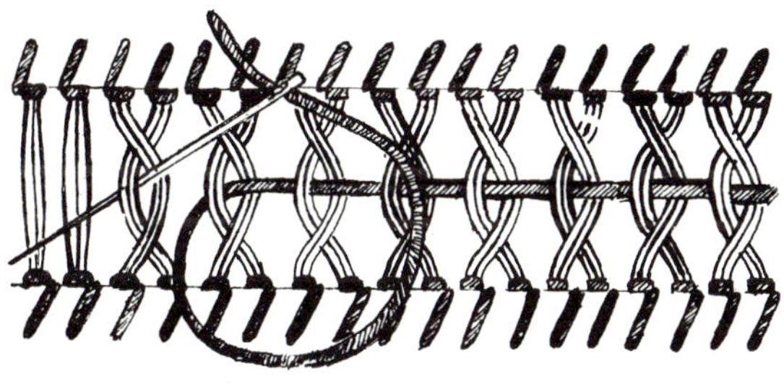
d

e

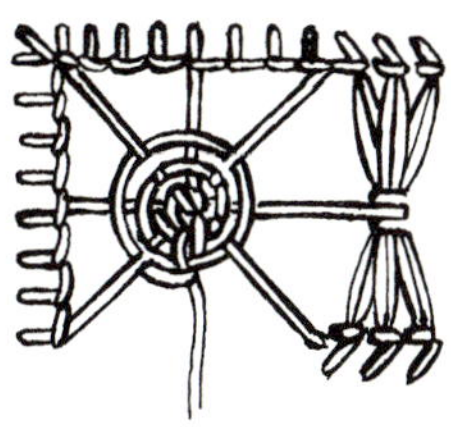
f
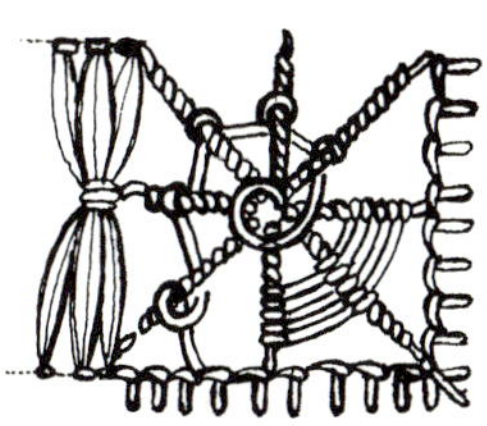

# *Rouleaux work*

This pretty and ornamental decoration is made up of a tracery of thin rouleaux (bias tubes) joined together by a traditional open-work stitch called faggoting (see page 18).

Tiny rouleaux first appeared in French peasant work, and this style of decoration was almost forgotten until it found its way into the stylish Parisian couture of the twenties, at a time when stitches were becoming up-dated and used in new ways and on a different scale. Its popularity increased throughout the thirties, and versions of it adorned glamorous ready-to-wear frocks.

This is an ideal technique for use on small, loose garments such as jackets and over-blouses, when the dress underneath is visible through the decoration. It is also ideal for decorative yokes, bands and small motifs intended for dress insertion.

Rouleaux decoration is usually worked in the same material as the dress, but you could use a contrasting colour of exactly the same fabric or create a light and shade effect by using both sides of satin-backed crêpe. Care in the choice of fabric is essential: the most pliable fabrics, giving perfect results, are lightweight and lingerie silks and rayons, moss, satin-back and plain crêpes.

**Making rouleaux** (a)
Cut several strips of fabric on the cross making them 1 in. (25 mm) wide. Cut the ends straight with the grain. Place the ends to be joined right sides to-

gether, with points projecting, and machine stitch them together. Press the seams open. Fold the fabric strip lengthwise, right sides inside, and machine stitch just $\frac{1}{4}$ in. (6 mm) from the fold. Stretch the fabric as you stitch. Trim away the raw edges. Insert a bodkin to its full length in one of the open ends. Secure it in this position by sewing through its eye and the tube opening using a fine needle and strong thread. Now draw the bodkin through the tube, so that the entire folded strip is reversed.

**A pinched rouleau** (b)
This method of stitching the rouleau gives it a pretty, bead-like appearance. Thread your needle with double cotton and push it through the centre of the rouleau from the back to the front. Now put the needle vertically behind the band and pull it through the loop, up and towards you, tightly. Pass the needle through the centre of the fold horizontally, and to the right of the knot just made, bringing it out $\frac{1}{4}$ in. (6 mm) to the left. When finished, the working thread becomes invisible.

**Decorative traceries** (c)
First make a pattern of the lines you wish the rouleaux to follow, marking them out on stiff paper or thin card. Baste the rouleaux over the lines and then work faggot stitches between them (see page 18). When completed, remove the finished section from the card, and it will be ready to attach to your garment. If further tracery is required, baste a new section to your pattern and proceed as before. Attach the tracery to the garment with more faggoting.

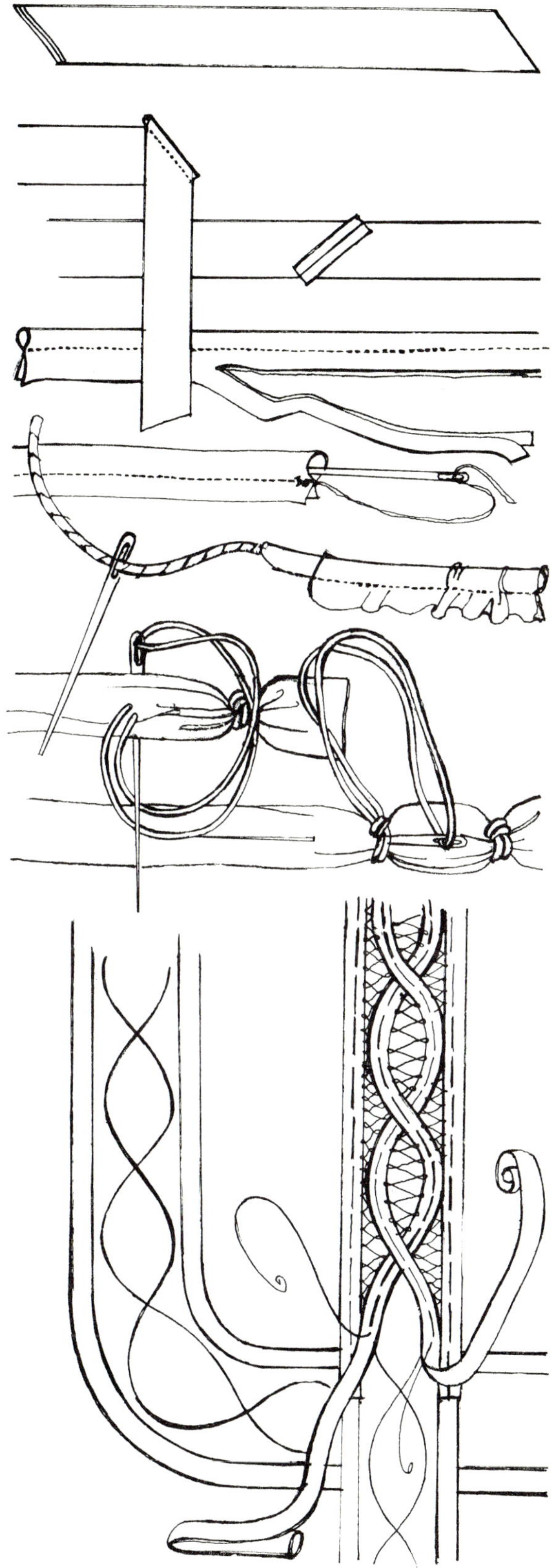

a

b

c

# *Couching*

Couching is one of the bolder embroidery methods. It is used to create decorative linear shapes that stand out from the garment in relief. The designs may be worked in a special couching thread or in a selection of cords and yarns of assorted thicknesses, textures and colour. String, chenille, knitting or rug wool, Russia or soutache braids are all suitable.

Fashion designers have recently been quick to appreciate this traditional decorative technique, and even the not-so-skilled dressmaker can use it to great effect, for couching looks good from any distance. It is fun, quick and easy to do. Couch a motif on a pocket or yoke, or make a wide border of curves and arabesques or an ornate pattern of spiralling leaves and flowers.

Use a simple side stitch over the couching thread, or a more decorative herringbone or blanket stitch, and remember that the stitching is intended to be visible. Use a thinner thread for the stitching than for the couching, and choose a contrasting colour for a more prominent effect.

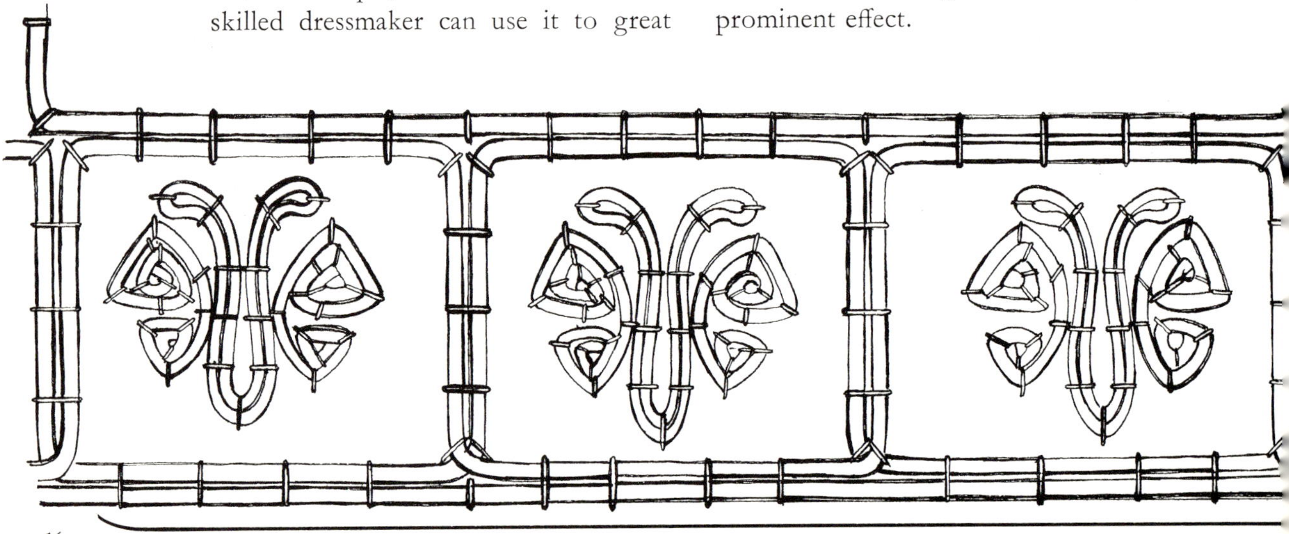

The characteristic pronounced outline of couching is often used to emphasize other decorative work such as appliqué or quilting. Patterns built up of couched metallic soutache braid can be used as a basis for *passementerie*, in which gold and silver shapes are filled with seed pearls and sequins on velvet appliqué (see page 58).

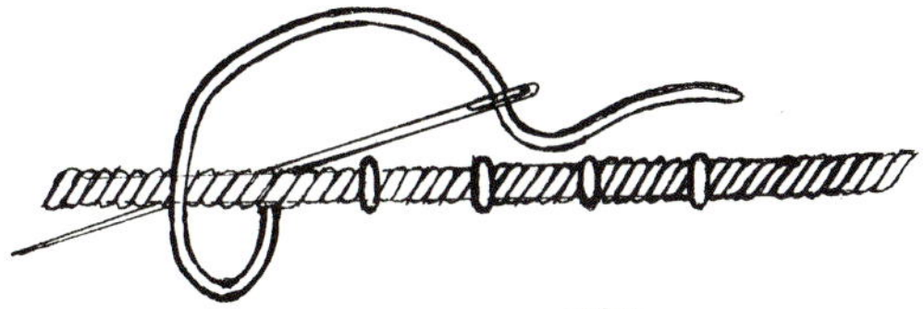

a

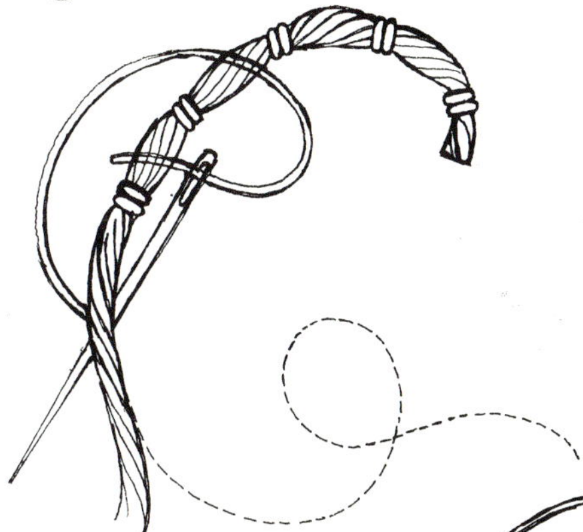

b

**Simple couching** (a)
Mark the design with tacking stitches. Lay the couching thread over the marks, leaving a $\frac{1}{2}$ in. (12 mm) end. Bring the stitching thread through from the back of the material at the beginning of the design. Make a stitch over the couching thread (a) and exactly at right angles to it. Bring the needle up again just over $\frac{1}{4}$ in. (6 mm) along the thread and make another small stitch across it. Repeat this even stitch at regular intervals until the design is complete. Cut the couching thread, allowing $\frac{1}{2}$ in. (12 mm) at the end. Pass this cut end through the fabric with the aid of a stiletto or darning needle, and catch it down. Fasten the other loose end in the same way.

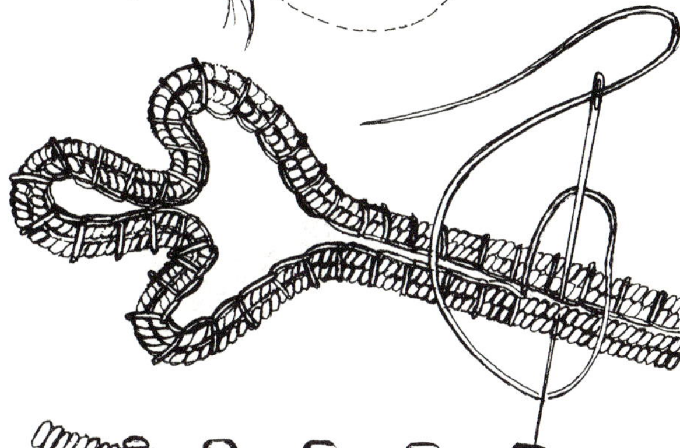

c

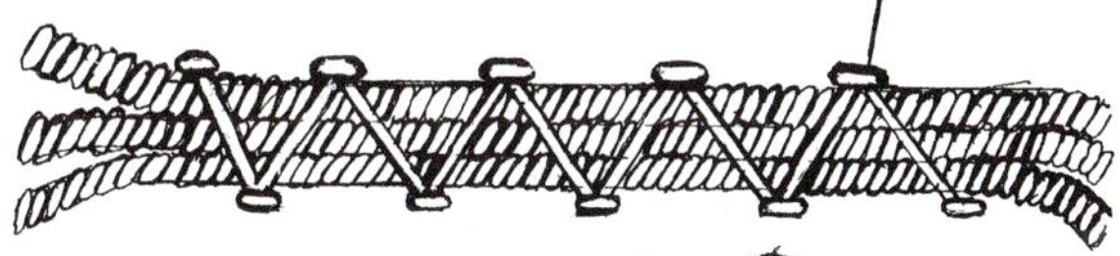

d

**Variations**
Experiment with double stitch (b), blanket stitch (c), and cross stitch (d) for more decorative effects. Whichever stitch you use, it is important that the couched pattern or motif itself should have a continuous regular and even flow.

# *Faggoting*

Faggoting is a method of filling in an open space with a decorative tracery of stitching connecting two pieces of fabric so as to allow a space between them. It can also be used in rouleaux work (see page 14) when it is used to join an openwork tracery of bias tubing, which is then stitched to the dress with more faggoting. Faggot stitches may be simple or twisted, with several traditional variations such as bar and pillar stitch. The technique of faggoting is old; the fashion value high. Originally it was confined to small-scale decoration on lingerie, fine blouses and dresses. The twentieth-century concept of fashion exploded traditional techniques, the scale altered, a greater variety of threads began to be used, and braids, ribbons, beads and jewel decorations were added.

**Preparing the fabric**

Turn and press the two edges of the fabric and tack them on to heavy paper, keeping them an even distance apart. If combining faggoting with rouleaux, tack the bias tubes on to a design drawn on stiff paper (see page 15).

**Twisted bar faggot stitch** (a)

Bring the thread from underneath one edge of the material and take a stitch directly opposite. Then take two to four loops over the bar of thread thus produced. The number of loops will depend on the length of the bar. Complete the stitch by inserting the needle at the point where it started. Slip the needle along $\frac{1}{4}$–$\frac{1}{2}$ in. (6–12 mm) inside the fabric edge and then work another twisted bar.

**Criss-cross faggot stitch** (b)

Starting at the bottom right-hand edge, bring the needle through to the right side close to the edge. Make the next stitch diagonally across from it from front to back of the fabric, making sure the point of the needle passes over the thread. Continue in the same way, with the needle passing over the thread each time. Keep the stitches an even distance apart – usually $\frac{1}{8}$–$\frac{3}{8}$ in. (3–9 mm) – although it can be as much as 1 in. (25 mm).

**Beaded faggoting** (c)

Use normal faggoting stitches, slipping the needle through a bead before each stitch.

**Rouleaux work** (d)

Join the rouleaux with any kind of faggoting stitch. The diagram shows a variation criss-cross faggoting with twisted bars.

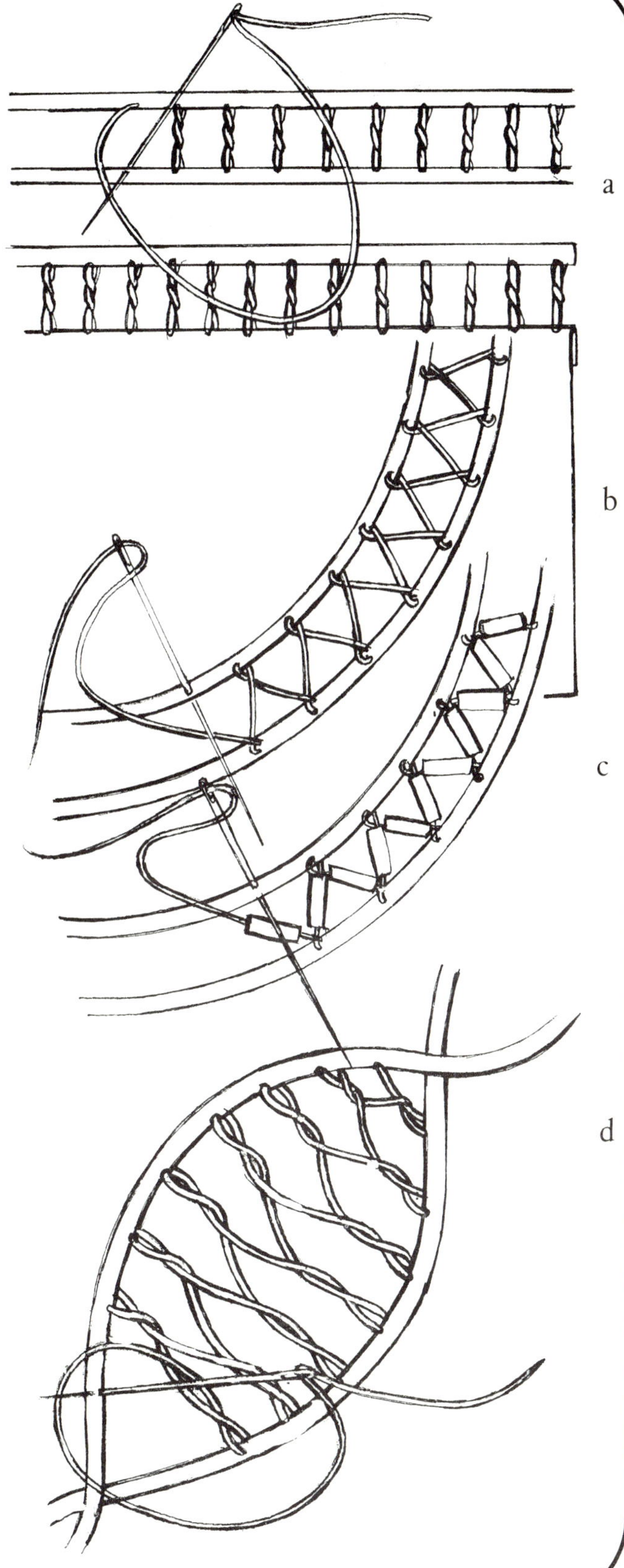

# *Smocking*

English smocking, as it used to be known, was a humble art. Not primarily ornamental, it was considered a convenient and flexible form of gathering which could not be replaced by any other form of stitchery. The style of the stitching took its character from the embroidery with which the garment was invariably trimmed. Smocking is an age-old technique, although modern versions derive mainly from the traditional Essex and Wessex smocks of nineteenth-century England.

Today smocking can be used on every conceivable article of clothing, and on almost any fabric ranging from rough tweeds and fine wools to veilings, voiles, silks, velvets, satins and crêpes. The choice of threads is almost equally wide.

It is wise to familiarize yourself with the traditional stitches and patterns, building up a 'smocking vocabulary' with which to formulate individual designs. These stitches include outline, cable, feather, chain and honeycomb stitches, with diamond, zigzag, wave and trellis pattern formations. These can be used in combination with embroidery – chain stitch butterfly or flower motifs, perhaps – to make original borders, yokes and waistbands.

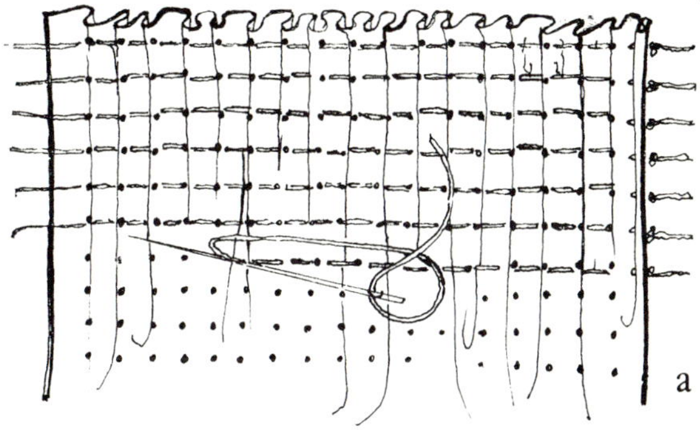

a

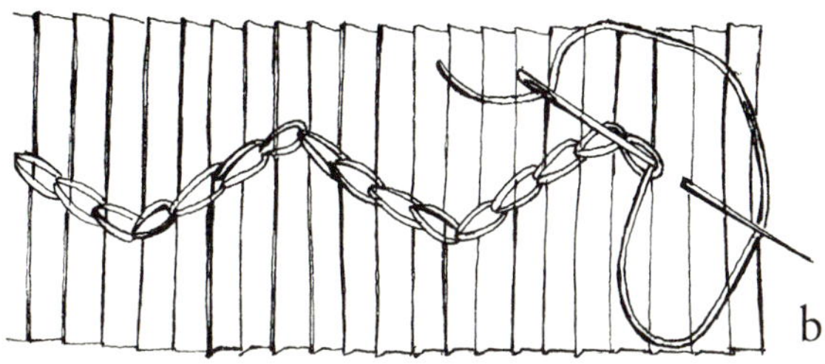

b

### Preparing the fabric

The smocking area should measure three times the desired width of the finished work. Using smocking dot transfers, mark rows of dots on the material with a warm iron. Gather the material using large stitches and coloured thread, passing the needle in at one dot and out at the next (a). These threads will be removed later. Draw up the threads to the right, pulling each thread individually and winding it on its own pin at the end of the line.

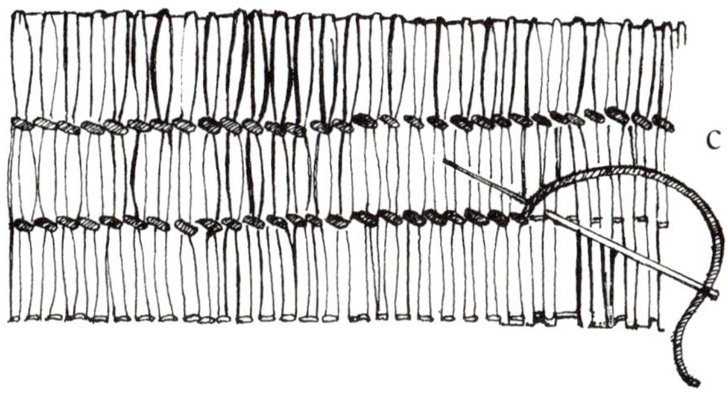

c

### Chain stitch in zigzag pattern (b)

Take up two pleats with every stitch, advancing one pleat each time.

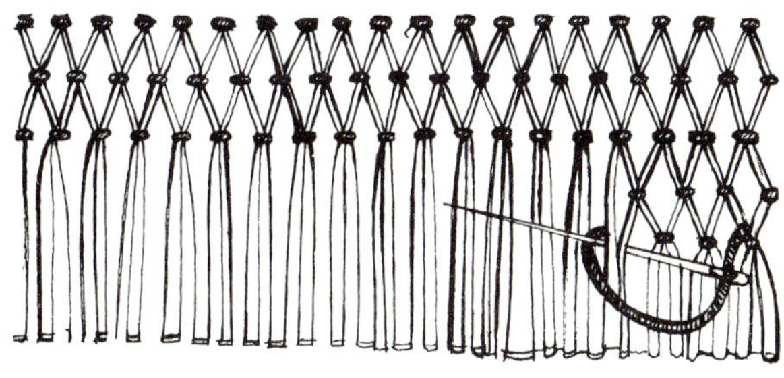

d

### Rope-stitched smocking (c)

This is one of the simplest stitches. Take up each pleat separately.

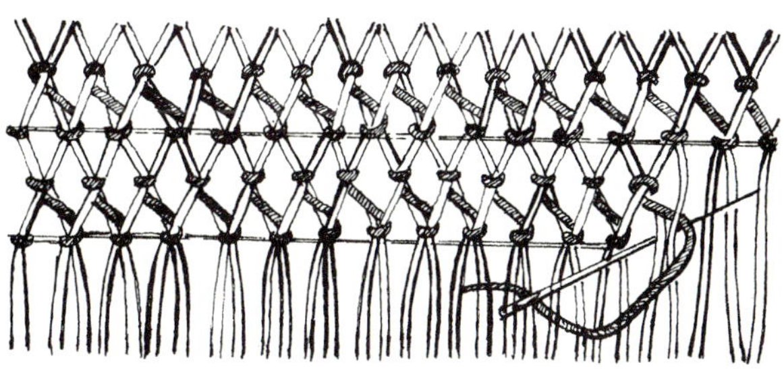

e

### Honeycomb smocking (d)

Work from left to right over alternate lines of dots. Drawing (e) shows one of the numerous decorative variations of this stitch.

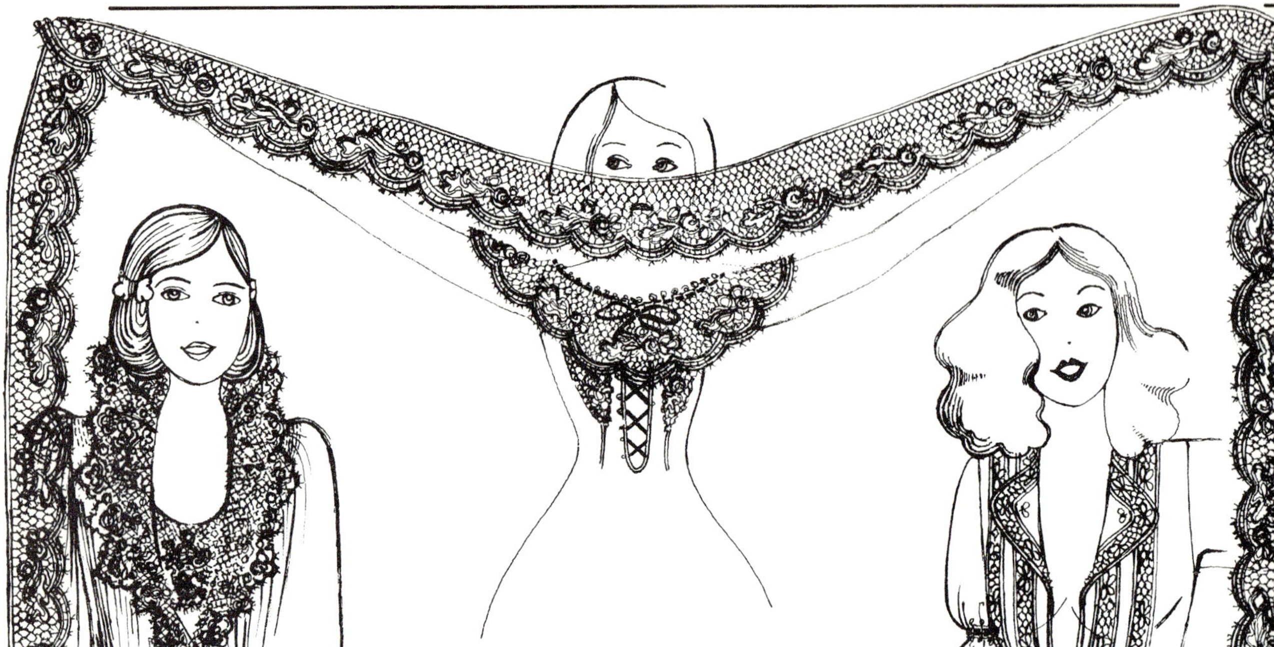

# *Lace trimming*

Lace, the feminine favourite of all time, is seeing a tremendous revival. The stores are full of modern laces in a host of colours reminiscent of the start of the century. In the stores there are delicate filigrees as well as heavy crochets and guipure, and in the street markets is such a plethora of antique edges, borders, insertions, flouncings and frilled edges to draw narrow ribbons through, that one feels almost compelled to wear them in one way or another.

Remember when choosing lace trimmings that they must launder in the same way as the fabric to which they are attached. Bear in mind that most modern laces contain synthetic fibres, while old ones do not.

**Lace edging**

Finish the raw edge by hemming or simply by turning and pressing it back. Lay the right side of lace against the right side of the garment and whip

stitch closely from the wrong side (a). Fold the lace down and press the seam on the right side.

**Gathered lace frill** (b)
To gather, pull up the floating thread at the selvedge of the lace. Turn back and press the raw edge. With right sides facing, lay the edge of the fabric fractionally over the lace edge, pin, tack and topstitch it in position by machine. Pull the same thread up slightly to ease the lace round curves (b).

**Lace strip inset** (c)
Mark the position of the insets on the right side of the fabric with chalk keeping exactly on the grains. Cut lace strips to the required lengths. Cut between the lines and press back the edges of the fabric along them. Then either pin each lace inset into position from the front and topstitch it in place, or fold the lace against the fabric, right sides together, and sew it with machine zigzag stitch (c). To finish, cut the raw edges of the fabric away almost to the stitching. Press on the right side.

**Lace appliqué** (d)
Choose lace with a pretty motif, lay it in position on the fabric and tack it firmly in place. Whip closely round the motif or topstitch on the trim edge. Cut the lace away close to the motif (d).

**Lace inset**
Work as for lace appliqué, but after closely whipping the inset and cutting away the extra lace, turn it face down and with sharp scissors cut away the base fabric $\frac{1}{8}$ in. (3 mm) from the edge. Turn the work and press it on the right side.

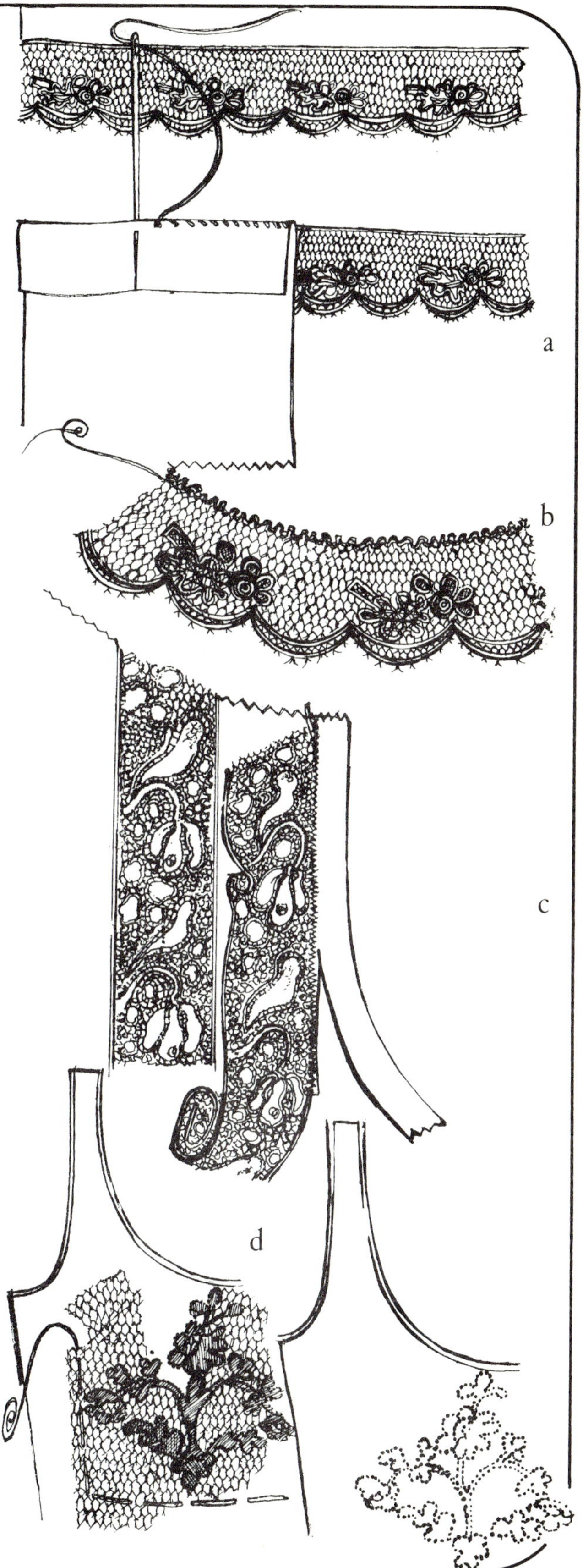

# *Fashionable fringing*

Fringing is fashionable, versatile and zingy. Why not incorporate a fringe in some novel way into your next dress? Try it out as a new way of finishing a hem or ornamenting a seam line.

Once you have mastered the simple forms of fringing you can do virtually anything with them. Swinging lampshade fringes, for example, need not be restricted to hems but can also be applied to pockets and seams or even threaded through dresses as they were in the twenties, creating patterns that emerge at various levels to swing with the movements of the body. The ends of fringes can be cut in scallops or in vandyke points and short fringing can be used in tiers.

Fringes fall into three categories – self fringes, knotted or tasselled fringes which need additional yarns, and applied purchased fringes (a).

### Self fringe

This is the simplest kind of fringing. First test your fabric to make sure it will fray easily. Loosely woven wools and linens are particularly successful. Cut the fabric along the grain and mark the depth of fringe required. Use a pin to help pull away the unwanted threads one by one. For extra thickness, cut a second strip of fabric 1 in. (25 mm) deeper than the fringe and prepare and pull out the threads as for a fringed edge. Attach the strip behind the first fringe with regular loose stitches. Hem stitch the top of the fringe so that it hangs in bunches (b), or simply to neaten it (c).

### Knotted fringe

Choose yarns to mix, match or contrast with the fabric. Cut pieces of yarn twice the length the fringe is to be. Using them in bunches (d), or singly (e), fold them in half and pull the loops through the fabric from front to back. Slip the ends through the loops and pull the threads tight. Space them close together or wide apart.

Make a trellis pattern with a long fringe by knotting (f), or a beaded fringe by threading a bead on to each group of strands before knotting them together (g). These fringes may be constructed on a folded edge or a hem, or even on a crochet base (g).

### Beaded fringe

You can make a very ornate fringe by threading several beads on a strong waxed thread and then looping the thread back to a larger bead. Use all kinds of crystal drops, metallic sequins, bugles and fluted beads, pearls etc. Continue adding more beads, repeatedly looping the thread back again (g).

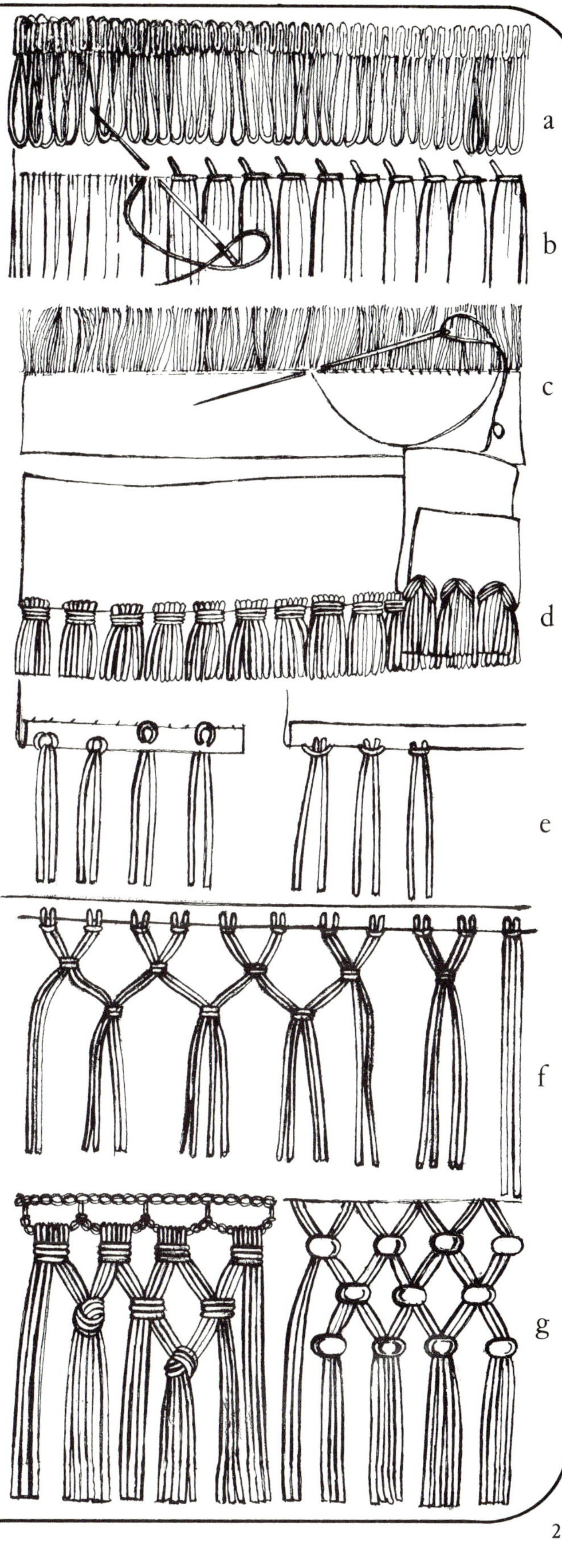

# *Tufted decoration*

Tufting is essentially a hand technique, thought to have been invented by our thrifty grandmothers in order to use up left-over yarns. It costs next to nothing, relying for its success on an interesting mixture of well-chosen colours and textures. During the late nineteenth century large areas of fabric were covered with patterned tufting in the fashionable colour combinations of the period. Brighter and more adventurous schemes are the vogue today, so why not try whole borders blending oranges and reds or mixing different shades of blue? For the beginner, a few small motifs will probably be enough; even a small amount of tufting can spell big fashion.

Tufted motifs are worked in a similar

way to a pompon, using a template of card, plastic or thin metal (see drawing). Unlike pompons, the tufted motif is stitched over the template on to a fabric background, so that when the threads are cut they produce a tufted effect in relief attached to the fabric itself.

### A tufted flower

You can buy a template or make one of cardboard. Lay it in position and embroider over it, working round the circle from the inside outwards and keeping the stitches at an even tension (a). Having worked one round, change the yarn colour and work a second round completely covering the first. Make a third round in the same way. When three layers have been worked, insert the point of a sharp pair of scissors into the middle of the flower and cut carefully round it (b). A tufted flower will gradually blossom in relief. Finish the motif by chain-stitching the stem and leaves (see facing page).

### Pompon

To make a pompon for use on the same garment, cut two circles of strong card the same size as the tufting template. Cut a hole in the centre of each. Place the card circles together and, using the same yarn in the same sequence of colours as before, thread it over and over the circles to make a fairly fat ball (c). Slip the point of a sharp pair of scissors between the outer edges of the card circles and snip right round them through all the layers of yarn (d). Draw a strong thread round the pompon between the cards, tie it tightly (e) and remove the card. Make a crochet chain to hang it on.

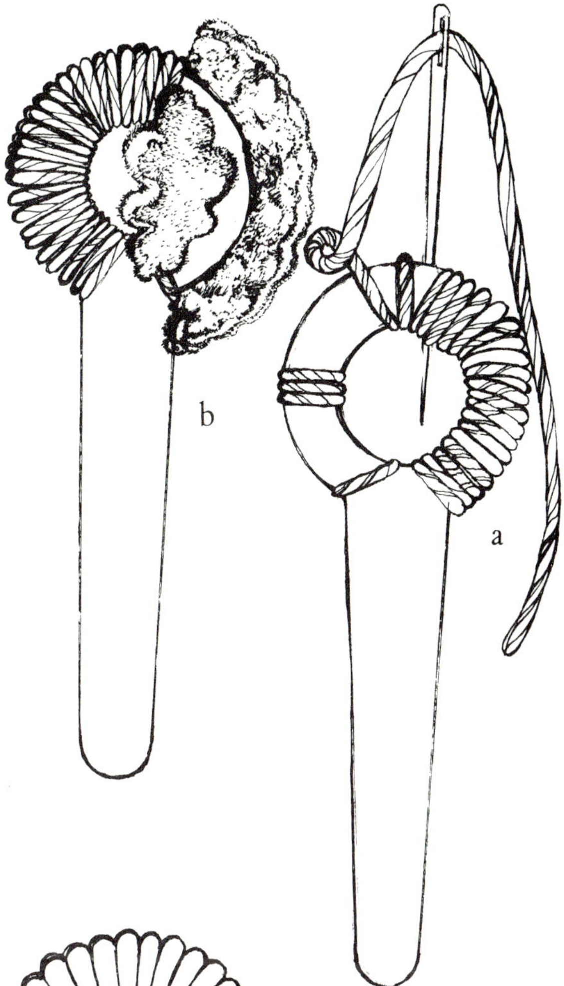


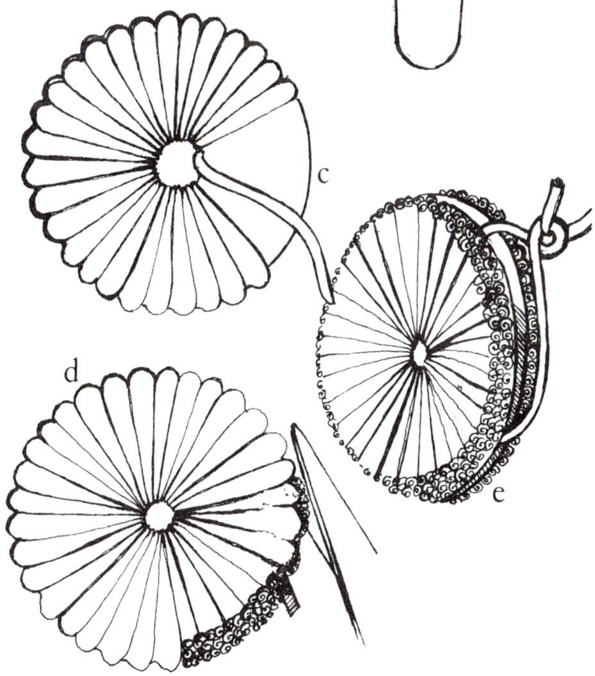

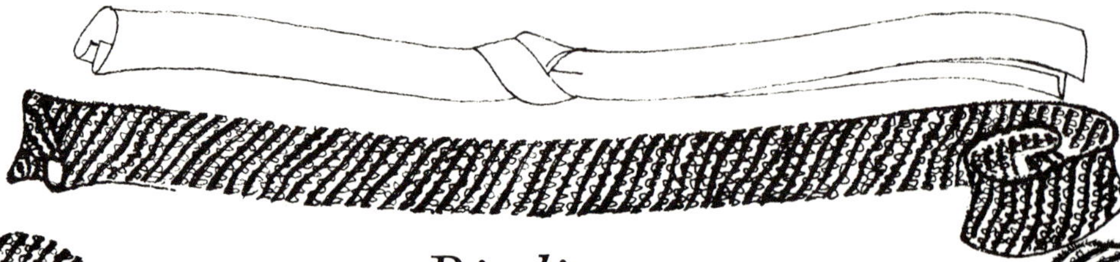

# *Bindings*

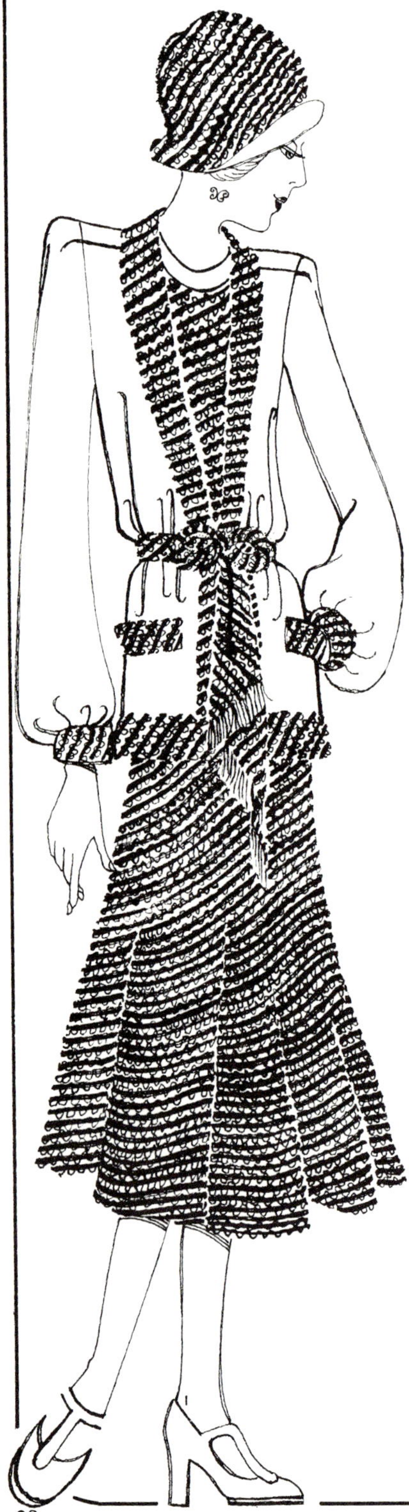

Edge bindings are not merely functional; they also serve a strict fashion purpose by accentuating the lines of a garment. Bindings on the edges, pocket edges, cuffs and hems of a jacket will add both strength and decoration.

Experiment with different colour schemes and bindings. If you are making a pants suit, for example, try black binding on a white jacket, and contrast this with black pants bound with the white material of the jacket to make a mix-and-match outfit.

Texture can have as much effect as colour. How about a satin jacket with a rolled tweed binding? Or a tweed jacket edged with satin? Take a tip from the thirties, and add a narrow binding of lingerie satin using the reverse crêpe side of the fabric, and this forgotten technique will play most effectively with light and shade.

Binding a raw edge in the same fabric not only gives a firm and decorative finish, but also acts as a facing. The finish of a bias strip binding must be immaculate, applied to the edge with great care. It is not necessary to flatten all bindings: the crease in a tweed binding may be encouraged, not pressed flat, and a rolled binding may be stuffed.

**Making crosswise strips**

Find the true cross by folding over a corner of your fabric so that the two selvedges are at right angles. Cut the resulting triangular section into parallel

strips, which should be double the width needed for the binding plus ½ in. (12 mm) seam allowance. Machine stitch the ends of the strips together on the straight grain of the fabric, forming diagonal seams (a). Press the seams open.

### Hand finished binding

Chalk a line to mark the position of the binding. Lay the strip against the mark, right sides together, and allowing a normal seam. Pin, then tack firmly before stitching (b). Fold the binding to the wrong side, fold in the seam allowance, and hand stitch (c). If the garment is to be lined, do not fold in the seam allowance but allow it to lie over the stitching and catch it down by hand or machine.

### Machine stitched binding

Work in the same way as for ready bought bias bindings. Mark the binding depth required on the garment, fold the binding in half, and press the raw edges inwards. Fold the binding strip over the raw edge and pin and tack it securely. Machine topstitch it into position from the front, ensuring that both back and front edges are caught in by the stitching (d).

### Double-folded binding

This is particularly suitable for silky and slippery fabrics where extra firmness is required. Cut a strip on the cross four times the width of the required binding plus seam allowances, and press or tack a crease along the centre (e). Pin and tack it into position, the raw edges towards the raw edges of the garment (f). Fold over the pressed edge to enclose the raw edges (g) and stitch it down on the wrong side (h).

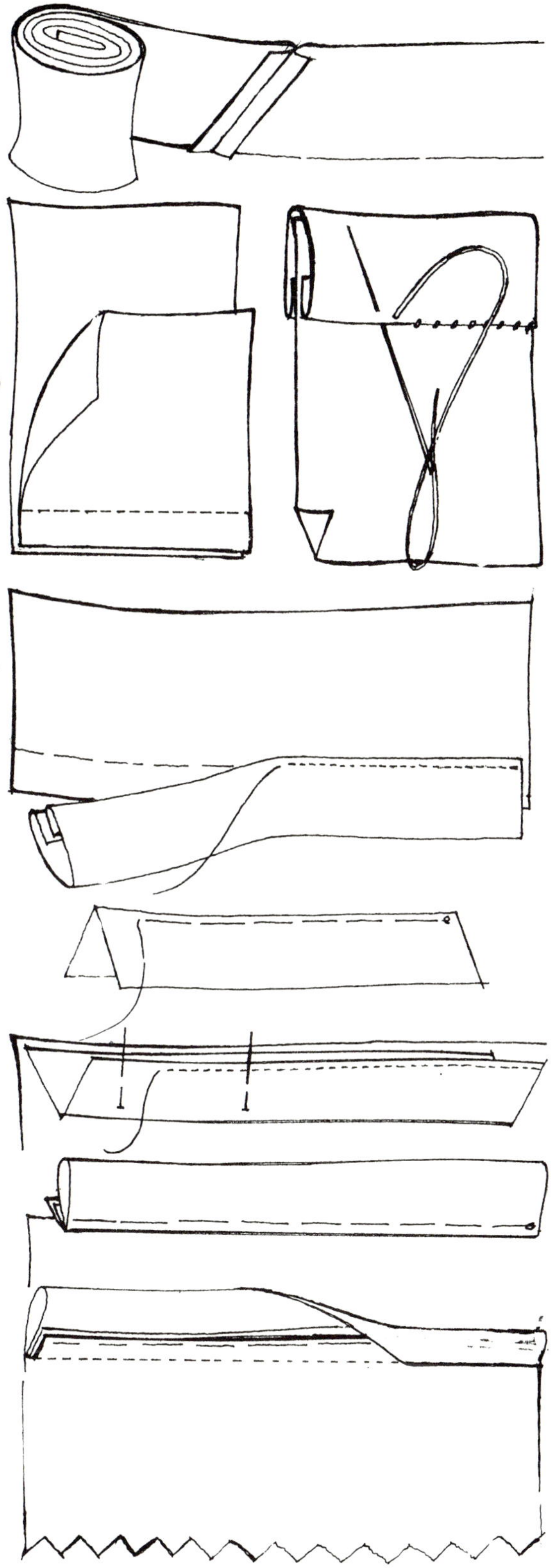

a b c d e f g h

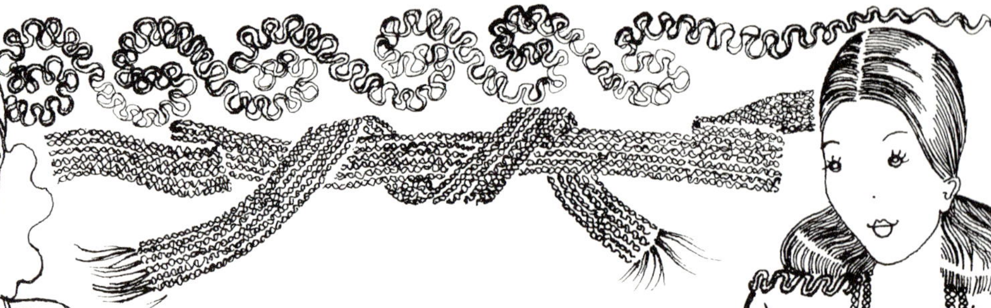

# *Braiding*

Tailored and military braidings are of an entirely different nature from the ornamental soutache described on page 32. They are used to emphasize tailored and masculine looks, outlining and at the same time taping and binding the edges of garments. They are knitted, either in matt wool or shiny art-silk surfaces. They may be bought flat, or ready folded down the centre to facilitate the binding of edges. They are suitable for accentuating the lines of immaculately tailored coats, jackets and blazers, but are equally adaptable to the feminine prettiness of soft crêpe pants or cardigan suits.

For richer effects, combine fancy textured braids by twisting them into ornate intertwining patterns which will stand out in relief. Full military style braiding can often be further decorated with froggings (see page 110), ornate buttoning, tasselling and so on. But the simple arrangement on a dress of just one single braid can be just as eye-catching.

### Braiding an edge

Prepare the braid by pressing it in half lengthwise. Measure half the width of the braid and tack mark the garment that distance from the edge. Lay the edge of the braid against the tacking and pin or tack it in place with the right side uppermost. Machine or hand fell it into position (a). Now turn the braid over the edge of the fabric and hand sew the second edge into position (b).

### Curved edges and corners

For curved edges, pin the braid in position, giving a little slack as you progress, right side uppermost. The slack will ensure that the edges do not curl. Stitch in the normal way (f). Pin the outer edge of each corner in position. Neatly fold the extra triangular-shaped piece to one side and stitch it down (g).

### Patterned border decoration of textured braid

Cut a template of curved repeats (c). Using sharp chalk, trace round the pattern on the right side of the garment, making certain that the pattern is even and regular. Pin the braid to the marking and fell it to the material (d).

### A braided motif

Mark out the motif on the cloth. Fix the cloth in a frame, and trace the braid around the pattern, pinning it out as you go (e). Start and finish the braid where the join will be least visible, possibly poking the ends through to the back. Tack the braid around the design and fell it in place. Remove the finished motif from the frame and press it lightly, using a cloth.

a

b

c

d

e

f

g

# *Soutache and Russia braids*

If you like fashion garments heavily decorated and ornately trimmed, a successful way of achieving this effect is to use braiding of all kinds. Soutache and Russia are types of braid designed to create outlines and patterns of curves, whirls, spirals, twists and scrolls. They are narrow, tubular and flexible, and are intended to curve naturally. Soutache is identifiable by its double ridge. Russia braid is a thinner, single cord; and the surfaces of both are wound with glossy thread. They are available in a wide range of colours including metallic gold, silver and bronze and can be used alone or combined with other trimmings to highlight a decorative effect. Laid-on stitched braiding may be used for borders in key or zigzag patterns, curved arabesques, scrolls and spirals, with linked corner arrangements or motifs, or it may be stitched in meandering vermicelli style. Fine wool, heavy tweeds, suèdes, doeskins, felts, nets and sheers – all these fabrics may be decorated in this way using different widths of braid or scales of design.

Soutache and Russia can also be used as embroidery, on the other hand, which lends itself to less formal arrangements such as ornamental bunches of flowers or abstract motifs.

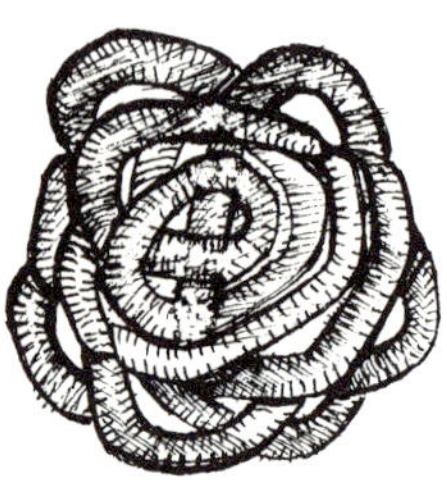

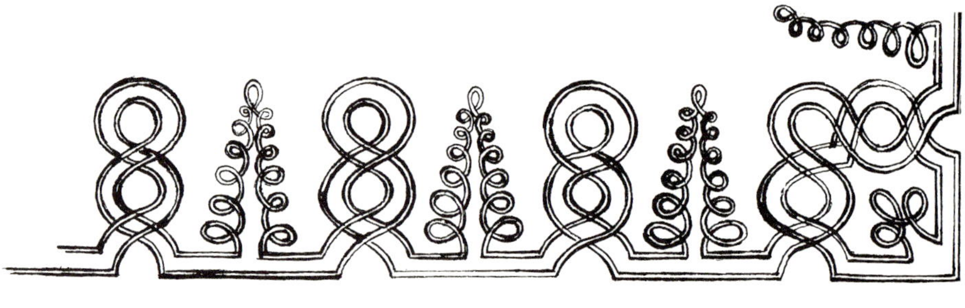

**Marking the design**

Outline the design with sharp chalk or pencil on the right side of the fabric. Test it by twisting and pinning the braid into position. When you are satisfied, stretch the fabric into a frame.

**Working the braid**

Braid is best worked by hand once the basic principles are understood. To start or finish, pass the soutache through the cloth with a large-eyed needle, and when applying a motif begin from the outside and work inwards. With most fabrics it is best to work soutache braid from the front, using loose back stitches down the centre channel of the braid. For a border, the soutache is passed through to the back at each intersection and back stitched as usual.

Russia braid should be lightly and invisibly catch stitched. When sewing sheer fabrics, work with the wrong side of the fabric uppermost, stitching the braid on from the back with one hand while guiding it into place on the right side of the fabric with the other.

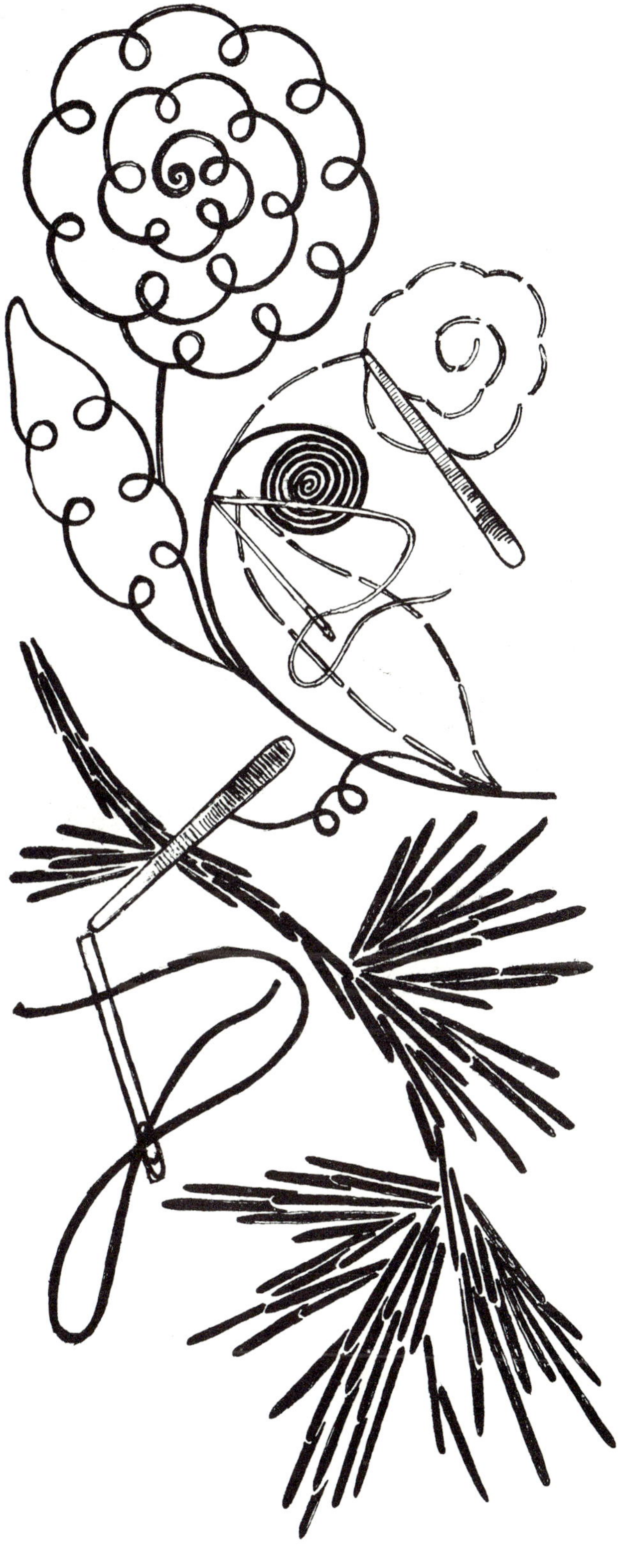

# *Woollen novelty edgings*

If you would like to trim a jacket, tunic or a scarf to slip on in the chill of a summer evening, why not use a simulated fur that you have made yourself? These amusing 'woollen furs' can be created with the aid of knitting needles or a crochet hook. Scan any knitting or crochet pattern books for loopy, bobbly or knotted textures.

**Knitted loop stitch** (a)
Cast on an uneven number of stitches.
*1st row* (wrong side) K1; * insert right-hand needle into next st., then with 1st finger of left hand at back of work take yarn loosely up over right-hand needle and down round fingers. Wrap yarn once round needle only and draw the two strands of yarn through st. on left-hand needle, slipping it off needle. Slip the two loops back on to left-hand needle and knit into the back of them. K1. Repeat from * to end.
*2nd row* Knit.
Repeat these two rows until the band is as wide as you want it.

**Crocheted loop stitch** (b)
Make this in thin or heavy yarns, or a double thickness of thin yarn. If you wish, you can cut the loops for a 'carpet' texture. Start by making a chain the length you need for the trim.
*1st row* 1 ch., 1 d.c. into 2nd ch. from hook, 1 d.c. in every ch. to end of row.
*2nd row* 1 ch., * insert hook into first stitch and pass yarn over index and middle fingers of the right hand, then over the hook. Drawing the loop through, then pass the yarn round the hook and draw it through the two loops on the hook. Repeat from * to end.
*3rd row* 1 ch., 1 d.c. into each stitch to end.
*4th row* As for row 2.
*5th row* As for row 3.
Experiment with other knitting and crochet stitches such as vandyked edging (c), twisted chain (d), and knotted crochet (e) to make more fancy, textured edgings.

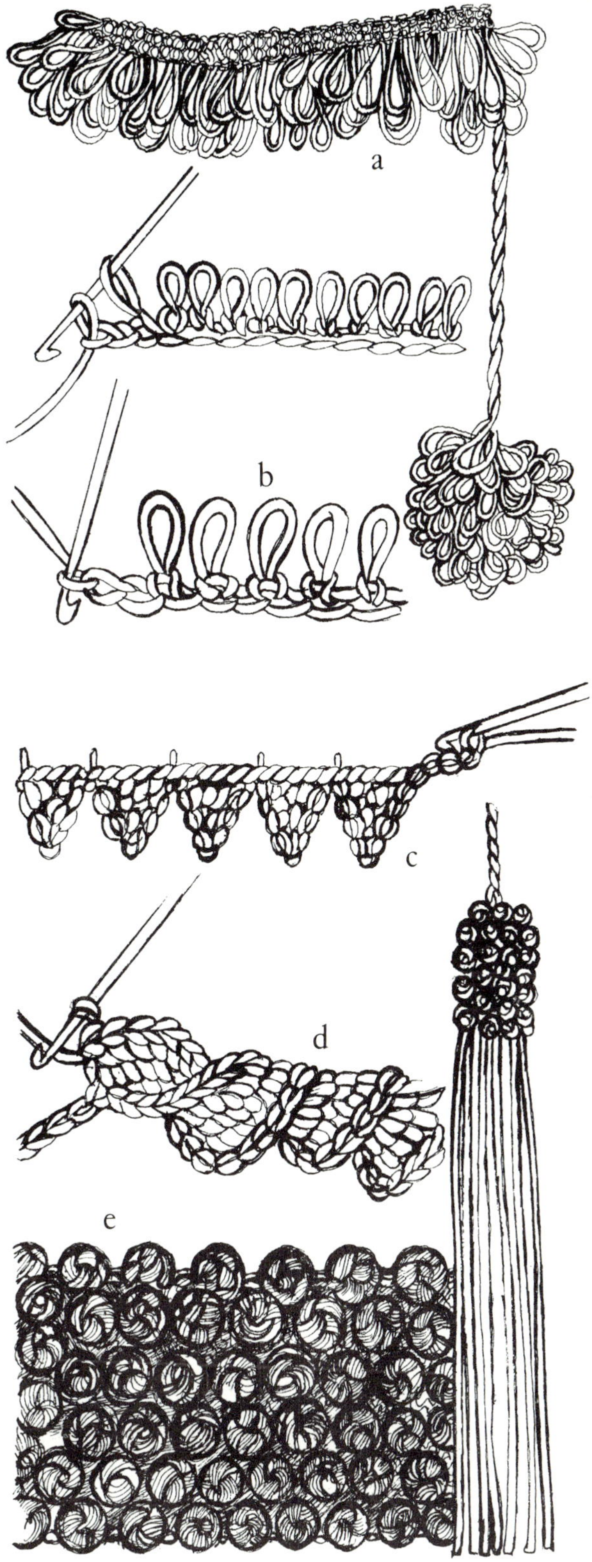

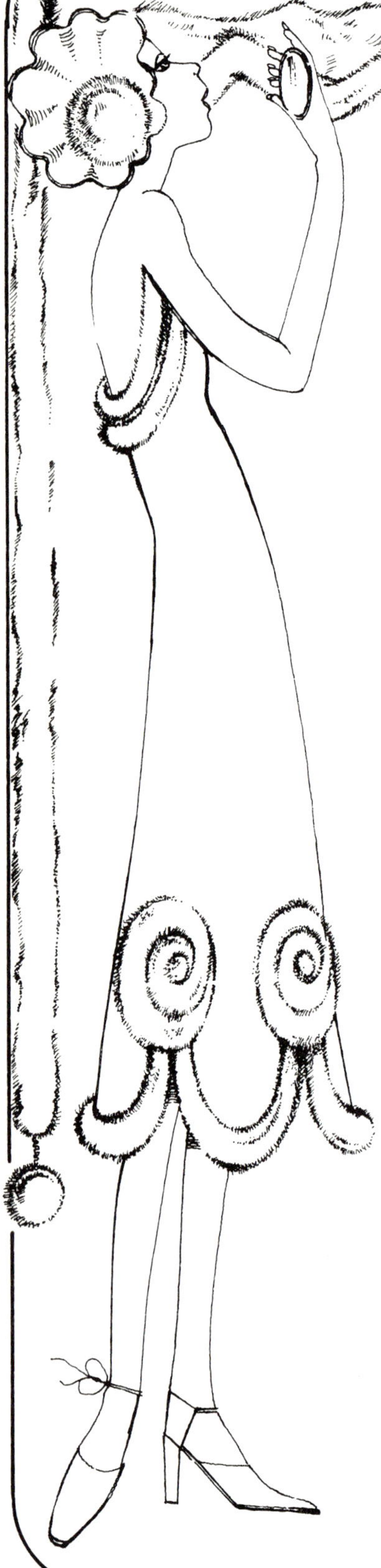

# *Marabou*

Change your mood with marabou. This soft feathery trim is lovely to wear next to the skin, on the inside of capes and evening coats, as a lining for huge, head-hugging collars, or peeping out of sleeve ends. It can be glamorous on shoulder capes or boleros, necklines or hems, and romantic as a boa to toss round your neck. Use it on gauzes, chiffons, satins and velvets to look extravagant and light as thistledown.

Marabou is obtainable by the yard or metre from major stores in a lovely assortment of colours. It can be used alone as a pretty decoration of zigzag, scalloped or crenellated edges, or with other feather trims such as vibrant cock and wispy ostrich for even richer effects. Experiment with setting diamanté or beads between rows and rows of marabou; nestling tiny flowers into the down; curling a strip of marabou into whorls, diamonds or other geometric shapes; making fluffy balls like powder puffs to stitch on your dresses; or combining several shades to make a whole rainbow.

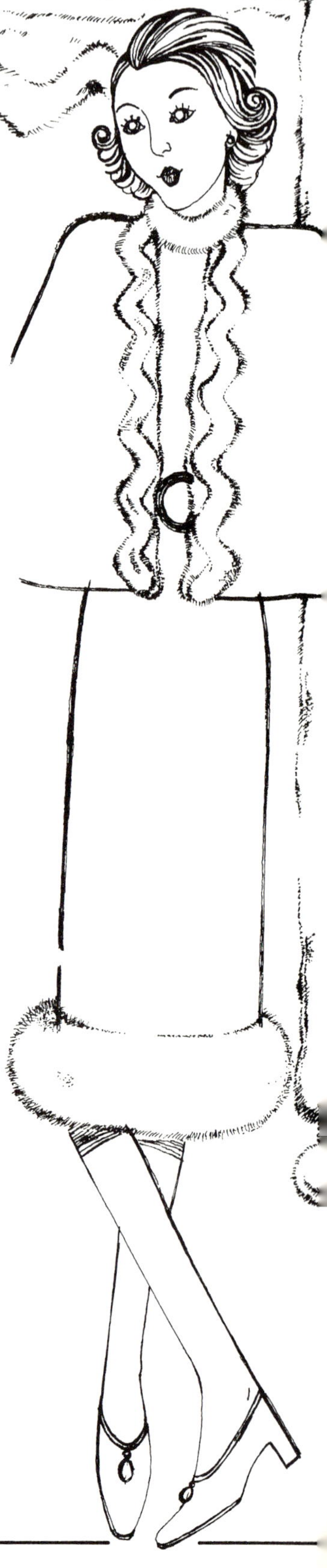

### Attaching marabou

Marabou is sold as a continuous fluffy strand with a central cord or tape for attaching to the fabric. The trimming is best carried out on a finished garment. Using either dressmaker's chalk or tacking stitches, mark the stitching line on the right side of the fabric. Pin the strip into position, making sure that the tape lies against the garment. Stitch the tape or cord firmly to the fabric using side stitch, slip stitch or back stitch. Make sure that you neither pull too tightly which will cause puckers, nor stitch too loosely in which case the strip will hang away from the garment.

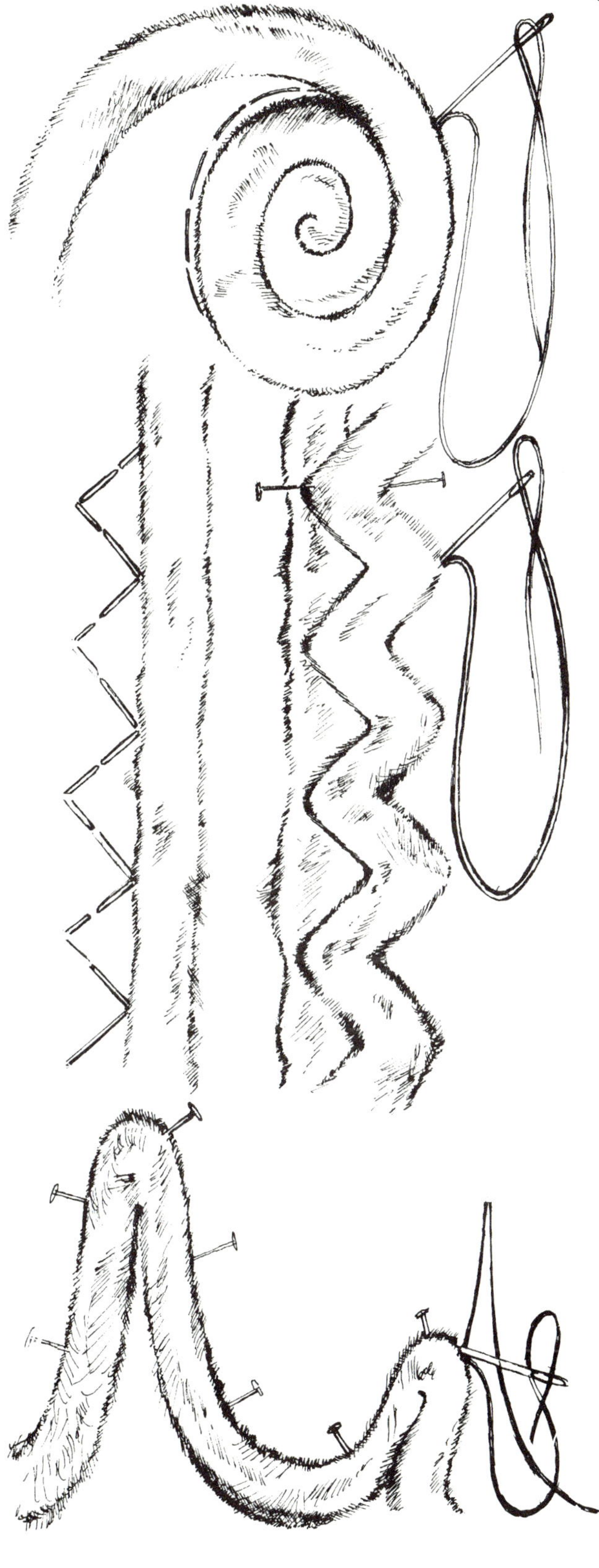

# *Strip edging*

Many simple and easy tricks with strip edging were familiar to our grandmothers, who deftly made infinite varieties out of ribbons, tapes and self strips of fabric. With imagination and skill, and often at no extra cost, you need never be at a loss for a pretty trim.

Try out your designs on a length of tape or paper the right width, pinning it out as you progress. For a three-dimensional effect you can pleat, plait, gather, concertina, tassellate, or use picot or vandyke edges. For flat treatments try making a chequered or lattice design, adding a little ribbon flower at intersections for extra prettiness (see page 98).

Traditionally used on baby clothes, millinery, blouses and little girls' dresses these trims are especially suited to miniature decoration, but they can be adapted to suit all kinds of moods.

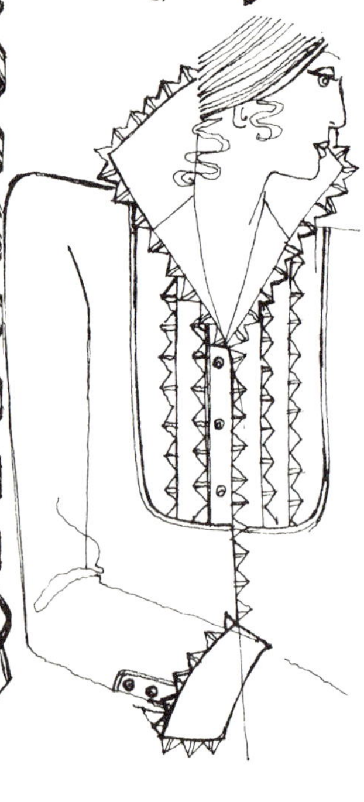

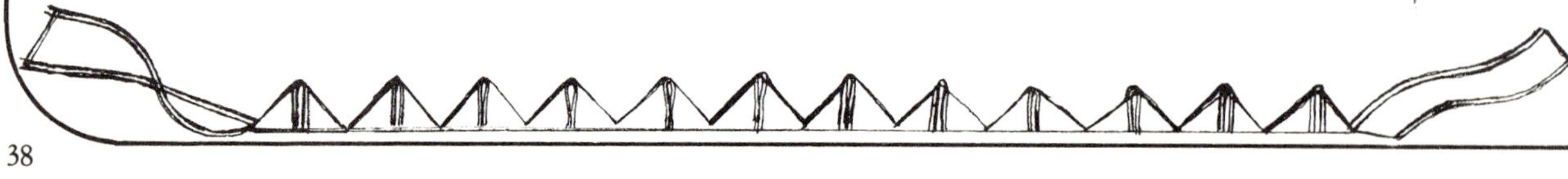

**Strip trimmings**
Cut several straight or crosswise strips of fabric, their total length about three times the length of trim required. Finish the edges with machine stitched hems or fringes (a), or fold the edges back to the centre, tubular fashion. Instead of fabric strips you could choose from the very wide variety of ribbons available and perhaps fold them into a picot edge (b).

**Centre gathers** (c)
Crease a fold down the centre of the strip. Run stitch by hand or gather it by machine before sewing it to the dress.

**Edge gathers** (d)
Make as above, the stitching line close to one edge of the strip.

**Zigzag gathers** (e)
First crease and press the strip down the centre or mark a centre line with chalk to help you space the stitching evenly. Sew the gathers in zigzag fashion.

**Box pleats** (f)
These pleats need strips three times as long as the finished trim. Cut several identical strips of card the width of one pleat to use as gauges. Lay the ribbon wrong side up on a flat surface. Fix the right-hand end to the surface with sticky tape and pleat the strip round the gauges, pressing or pinning the creases in place. Make a line of stitching along the centre.

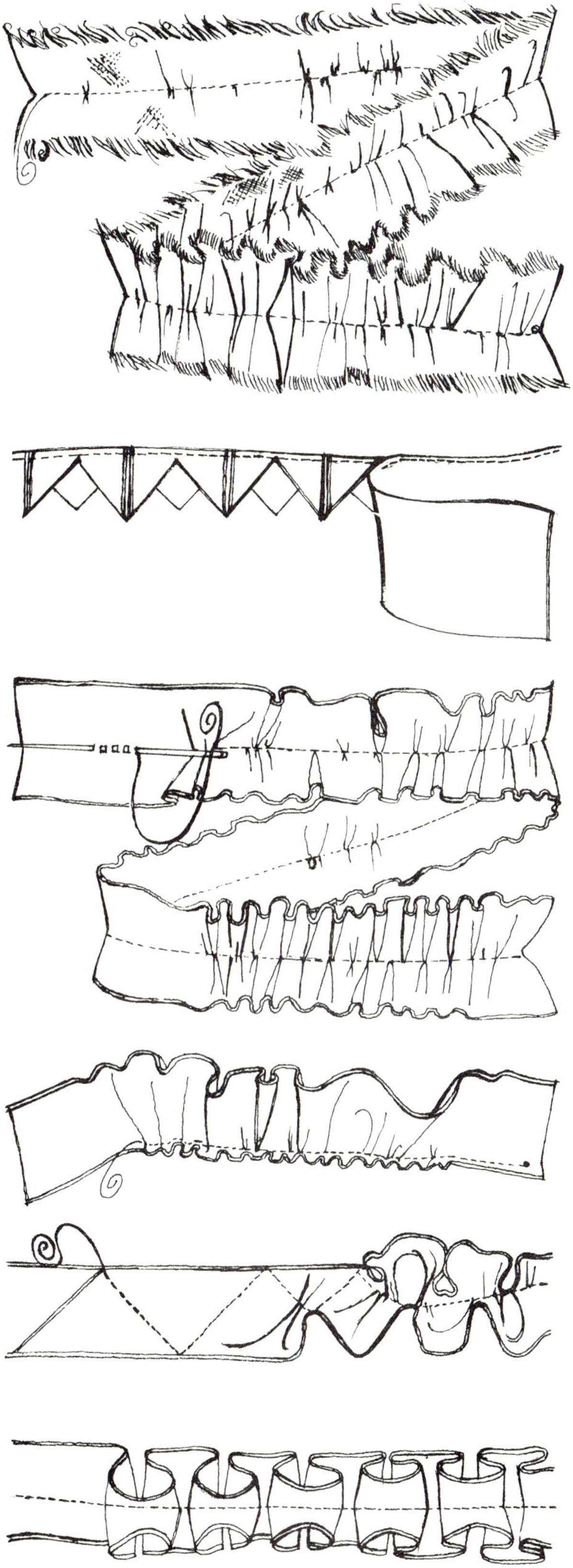

a b c d e f

# *Scallops*

There is a kind of scallop to suit every garment. Scalloping reached the height of popularity on dresses in the twenties and a revival came in the wake of such films as *Bonnie and Clyde, The Great Gatsby* and *The Boy Friend* through which Twiggy inspired the dress industry to produce a plethora of pretty scalloped dresses.

Scallops may be an integral part of the line of a dress or used to decorate hems and edges in a variety of shapes and finishes. The method of finishing the scallop is all-important to the design of the dress and is chosen to suit the fabric. The most common finish is the normal faced scallop, but the facing may also be reversed to make a decorative top-facing and finished with topstitching on the right side. You may choose to make narrow pipings or bindings for outlining the scallops or to edge them with buttonhole stitch. Scalloping on an automatic machine, though limiting the scallops to about $1\frac{1}{4}$ in. (30 mm) across, adds a very professional touch to children's clothes, nightwear and blouses.

Scallops need not be confined to a single shape; they can be round or ovoid, and the two shapes may be combined very prettily. An interestingly uneven scalloped hem can be made with alternate shapes hanging lower than the others.

All manner of fabrics are suitable – woollens, firm silks, taffetas, failles, satins, satin organzas and cottons.

**Faced scallops on a hem** (a, b)
Measure round the hem and divide it into an equal number of widths. Make a

scallop template the size of one width, and chalk the scallops round the hem on the wrong side of the fabric. Pin and tack the facing to the scallops, right sides together. Machine stitch along the chalk lines, back stitching the point of each scallop to strengthen it (a). With sharp scissors trim the fabric away to within $\frac{1}{8}$ in. (3 mm) of the stitching, snipping hard into each corner. Turn the facing to the wrong side and tack round the scallops on the right side (b). Press on the right side and remove the tacking.

**Top-faced scallops** (c)
Start in the same way as for faced scallops, but lay the facing and fabric wrong sides together before tacking. Machine stitch and trim the scallops as before, then turn the facing to the front of the garment. Trim the facing to an even depth, turn the edge under $\frac{1}{8}$ in. (3 mm) and pin and topstitch it in position (c).

**Piped scallops** (e)
Cut a bias strip of contrasting fabric $\frac{1}{4}$ in. (6 mm) wide to make $\frac{1}{8}$ in. (3 mm) piping. Press the raw edges of the strip to the centre. Right sides together, tack one edge of the strip to the cut edges of the scallops (d). Press the binding down and over the scalloped edges. Topstitch from the right side to catch the seam allowance up.

**Buttonholed scallops** (f, g)
Mark top and bottom outlines for the scallops on the right side of the fabric but do not cut them. Run stitch along the edge, and fill in between the lines with long and short stitches as a padding. Work over the padding with buttonhole stitches keeping the stitches close together. Trim away the extra fabric.

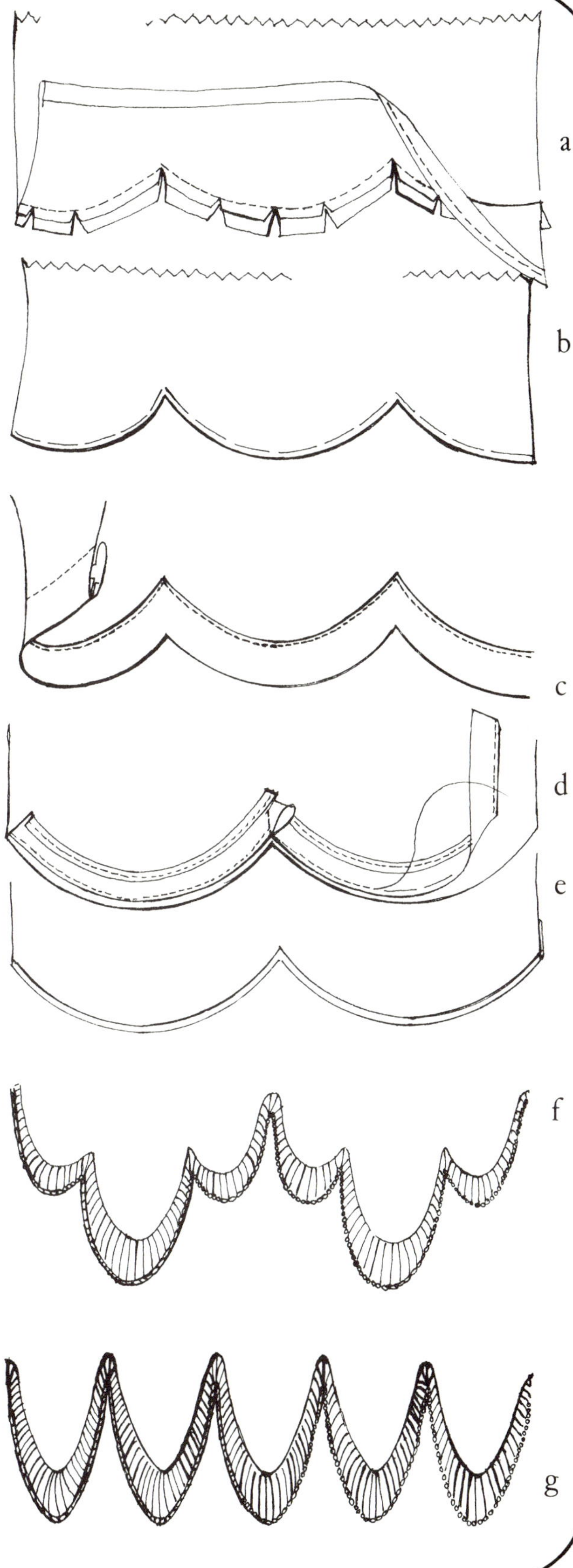

# *Embroidered edges*

If you find embroidery fun, you will discover unlimited scope for using hand-finished edges in fashion sewing, for there are so many simple, traditional stitches that can be adapted imaginatively to provide pretty and durable edgings.

Edge embroidery finishes are best carried out on simple, dressmaker garments that have simple facings and no interlining. Buttonhole stitch, cross stitch and their many variations, can be used in combination with other embroidery stitches or developed into more complex embroidery patterns. They can often be adapted to make embroidered borders for use on other parts of the garment. If you then decide to make a tasselled cord (see page 104) as a belt or fastening, twist both cords and tassels from embroidery yarns, to give the finished look a unified character.

### Stitching over a folded edge

Decorative edge finishes are best made over a folded edge. The main stitches used are buttonhole stitch, cross stitch and overcasting.

To make buttonhole stitch (a) start by bringing the needle through from the back, passing it between the turned-up hem and the garment, and bringing it out at the left-hand corner of the folded edge. Insert the needle $\frac{1}{4}$ in. (6 mm) in from the edge, passing the loop of thread round the point of the needle. Work a second stitch, inserting the needle $\frac{1}{8}$ in. (3 mm) to the right $\frac{1}{4}$ in. (6 mm) from the folded edge. Pass the loop of thread round the point of the needle once more. Continue in this way, working the stitches the same distance apart. Create your own variations by making the stitches close together or further apart, by using a mixture of long and short stitches, or by making them slant or even cross. Any of these variations may be worked on groupings of different colours.

### Stitching near the edge

Crease the hem allowance or facing to the inside and tack $\frac{1}{2}$ in. (12 mm) from the folded edge. Any number of decorative embroidery stitches may be used for a border, but chevron, fishbone, cross stitch (b) and feather stitch (c) are particularly suitable.

If you wish you can build up more elaborate patterns combining several stitches. Lazy daisies with fly and chain stitch (d) are all suitable ingredients for a more complex design.

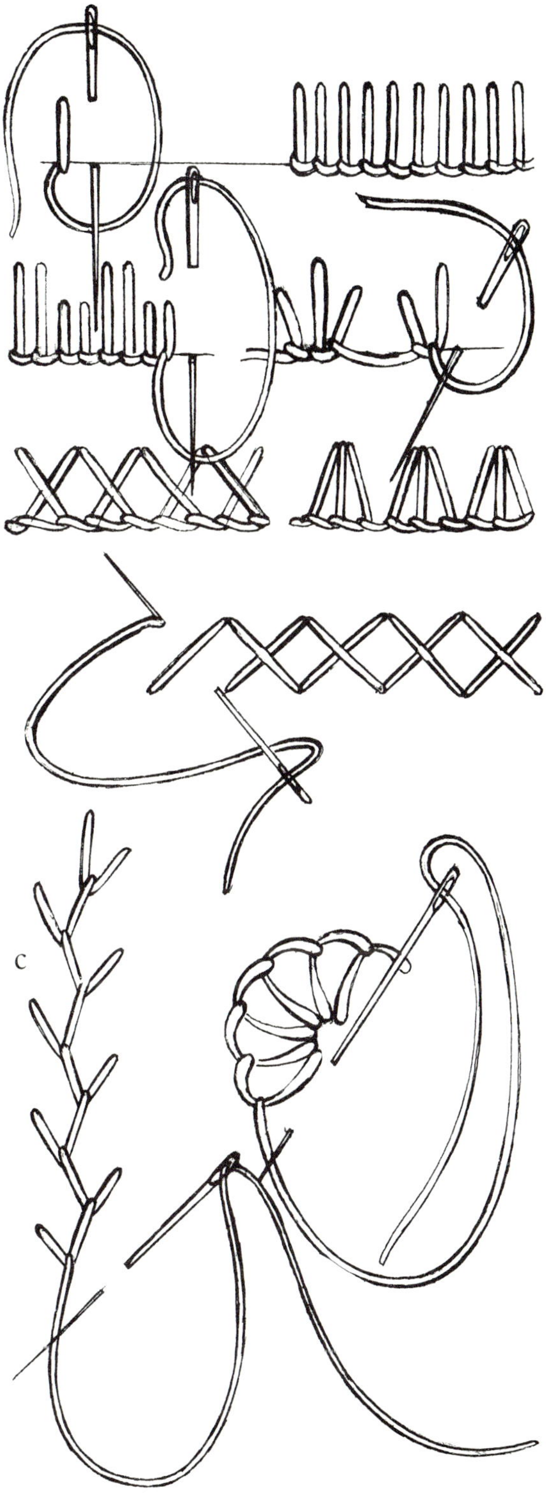

# *Machine embroidery*

The folk costumes of eastern Europe and Russia have had a strong influence on contemporary western fashion. The lines of the Cossack tunic, the peasant skirt and Slovakian blouse are very much in accordance with the shape of clothes worn today; and the peasant embroideries with which these clothes were so abundantly decorated lend themselves perfectly to free interpretation with the aid of a modern automatic machine, enriched by the occasional use of hand embroidery stitches.

In order to design successful embroideries, it is essential both to become familiar with the stitching possibilities of your machine, and to get to know the characteristics of folk embroideries, so that you can combine them to produce simplified but instantly recognizable versions. Slovak and Russian embroideries are by tradition rich in colour and geometric in character, using regular motifs, stylized borders and simplified lapels.

These Russian style tunics illustrate the uses to which embroidered panels, yokes, bands, cuffs and neck-pieces can be put to achieve a fashionable peasant look. The embroidery is carried out on the pattern sections before the garment is made up.

**Using automatic machines**
Automatic machines vary slightly as to the stitches they are designed to produce, the most useful being lines of decorative patterns. Fill whole areas with parallel lines of patterns or work them as decorative outlines to seams or tucks.

Before beginning to embroider, make sure the bobbin is correctly wound and the tension accurately set. If you have a twin-needle machine you can work the pattern in two colours or dual shades of one colour. After stitching a straight patterned line, make a sharp corner by stopping the stitching with the needle at its lowest point, lifting the pressure foot and turning the fabric. Replace the foot before continuing. Ease the work through carefully when stitching over bumps and avoid bending or breaking the needle.

A special gadget will allow your pattern to be worked in a circle with the work inserted into a hoop, and often a special foot is provided which will apply raised cordings. Some machines will stitch scallops, which make an unusual and effective edge trim on a single layer of fabric (see page 42).

The ideal fabrics with which to make peasant tunics, blouses or shirts are jewel-coloured Irish linens, bright cottons and white muslins, which you can cover in assorted coloured embroideries.

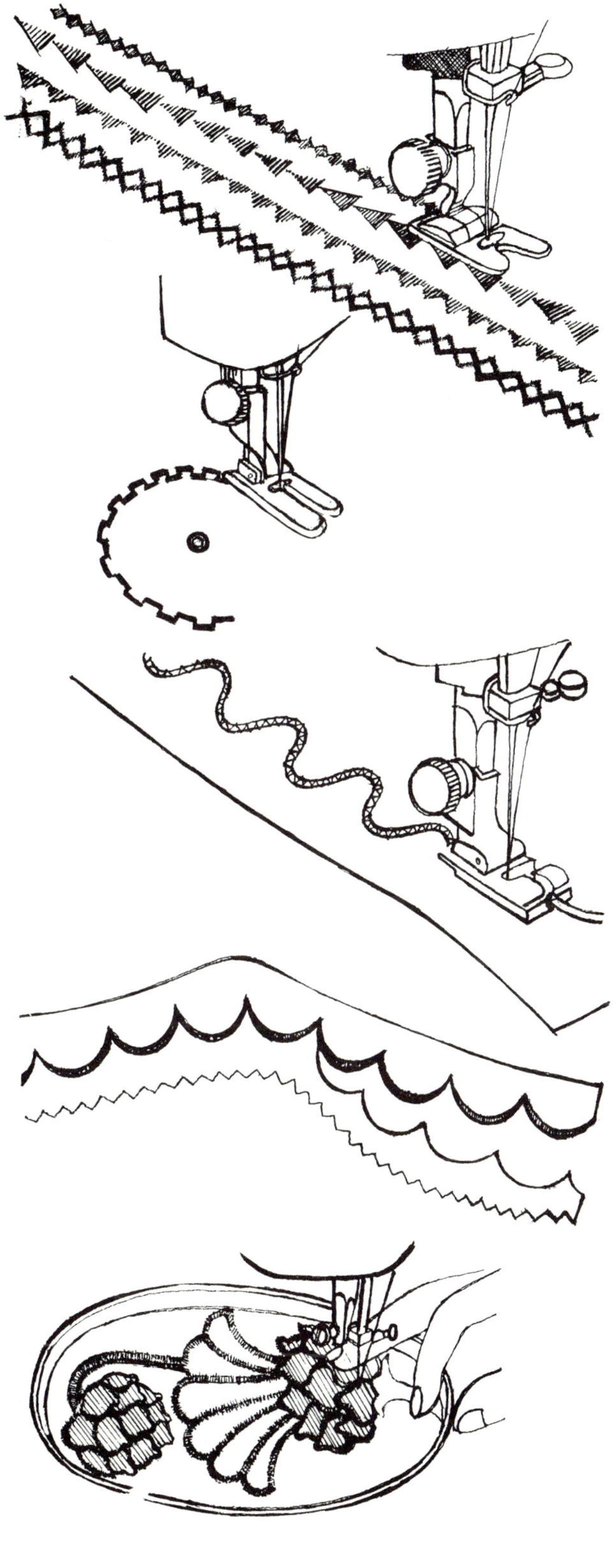

# Cutwork motif

Traditionally cutwork is one of the most effective embroidery methods used in dressmaking, as the open and solid parts of the design create a marked contrast. It looks ornate, but is actually quite simple to achieve. 'Richelieu' is the traditional name given to this style of work, characterized by its outline of blanket and buttonhole stitches, worked in open patterns separated by bars of thread which hold the pattern shapes together after the plain fabric sections have been cut away.

A single section or border of cutwork will make a delightful feature on a dress or jacket. Be severe or frivolous; the basic idea is versatile and with ingenuity and a little experience it is simple enough to change the look of cutwork to achieve quite different effects. Instead of using a matching thread in the traditional way, choose a contrasting one. Or try putting the finished cutwork over a section of differently coloured fabric so that you can see through the open embroidery work, thus heightening the relief.

Although cutwork is best suited to linen and similar types of fabric – favourites with Italian designers whose embroidered linen models are so distinctive – you can use other fabrics once you have mastered the technique. Until then, however, embroider small individual sections such as a pocket and collar, which can then be applied to a finished garment. Those with more experience can create a fairy-tale look for the evening using crisp organza, outlining the tracery cutwork with seed pearls sewn on from the back. Cutwork sewn in gold or silver thread is also very pretty for evening wear, but difficult for the beginner as it should always be worked in an embroidery frame.

**Basic cutwork**

Mark out the design in chalk and then run stitch all the outlines (a). Pad the more important areas with filling stitches, and work regular blanket or buttonhole stitches over the top (b). Less important shapes (c) should be blanket stitched without filling. Using sharply pointed scissors, cut out the inside of the worked shapes and then stitch bars across open spaces (d). Cover the bars with blanket stitch. If you are using a very intricate design, you should make some bars in order to hold the design sections together before you start cutting out. Traditionally, cutwork is confined to these few stitches, but nowadays other decorative stitches can be added as required.

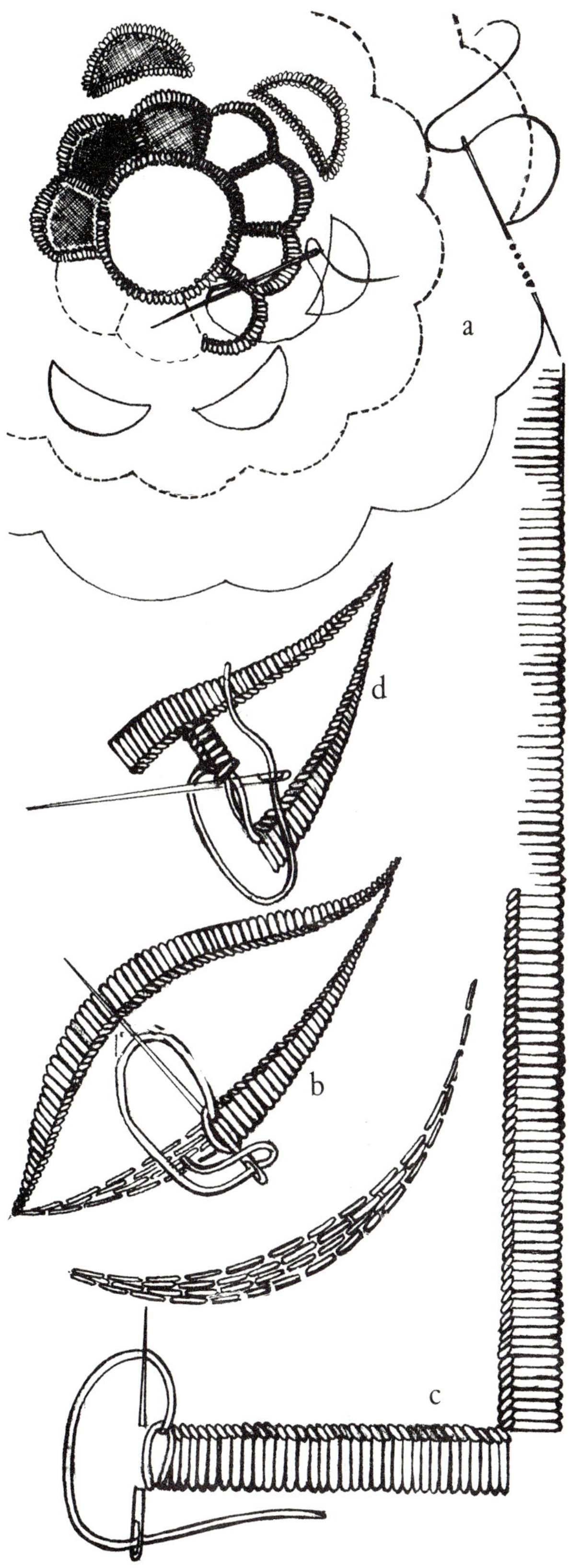

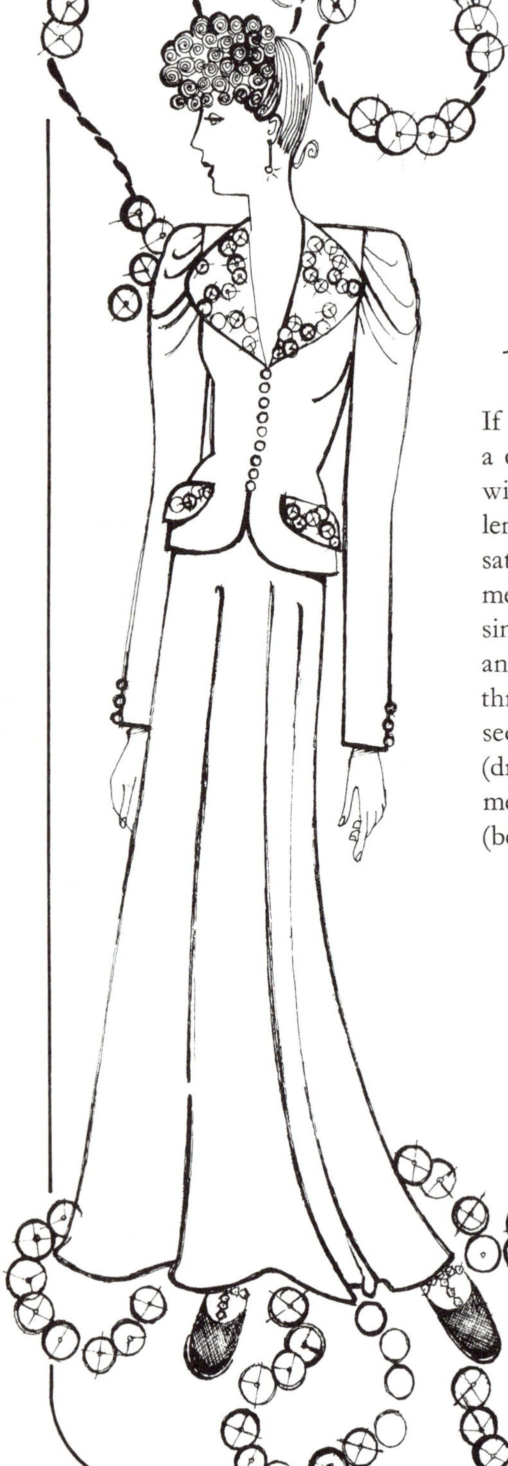

# *Metallic embroidery*

If you enjoy embroidery, why not cover a collar, sleeves or an entire dress front with heavy metallic embroidery? It lends itself particularly to shiny velvets, satins and taffetas sewn with couched-on metal braids, chenilles, metallic threads, simulated metal sequins, silvery bugles and brass beads. Try side stitch in gold thread with groups of three or four gold sequins worked on Prussian blue velvet (drawings above and right) or simulated metallic paillettes on a gold lamé fabric (below and left).

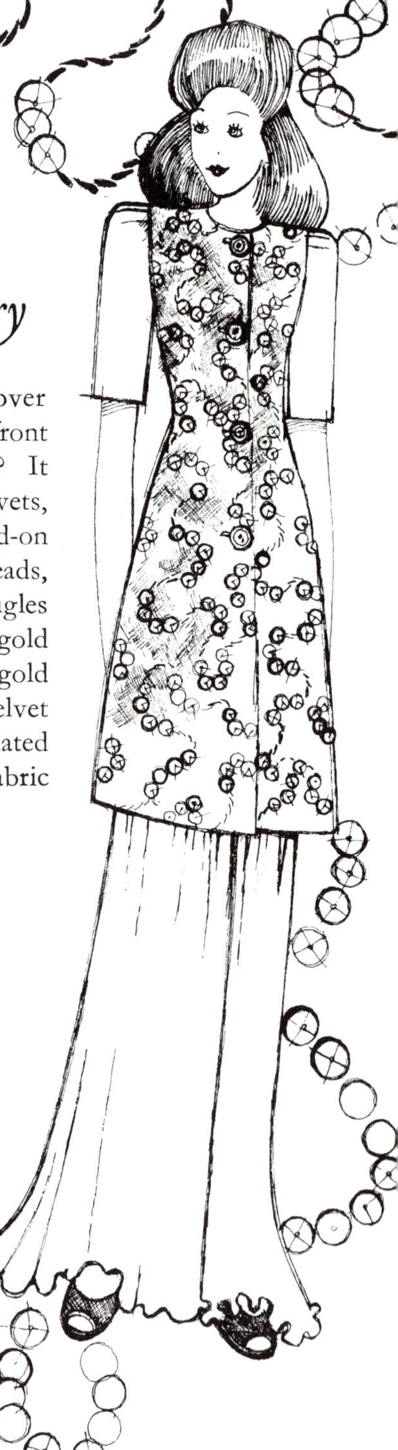

### Preparing the fabric

Select the paper pattern piece for the section to be embroidered and, using the drawings opposite, trace a pattern of curves on to it. Lay the pattern piece on the fabric and cut it out, allowing extra fabric for shrinkage caused by the embroidery. Back the fabric with flannel-type domett or mull. Transfer the curved design to the right side of the fabric (see pages 53 and 73). Work the design in back stitch and paillettes (see page 72) or single sequins (page 68) or with sequin strips. Keep sequins and paillettes away from the seam allowance, adding any final detail after the garment has been made up.

### Large areas of embroidery

Lay the fabric on a corresponding length of backing fabric and tack them together securely. Mark out the pattern sections, but do not cut them yet. Chalk the design on to the fabric where required and trace it out with small running stitches. Now work the embroidery, finishing ½ in. (12 mm) away from the seam lines. Check the pattern pieces against the original markings and make any adjustments before cutting out. Make up the garment in the usual way and finish off the embroidery near the seam lines.

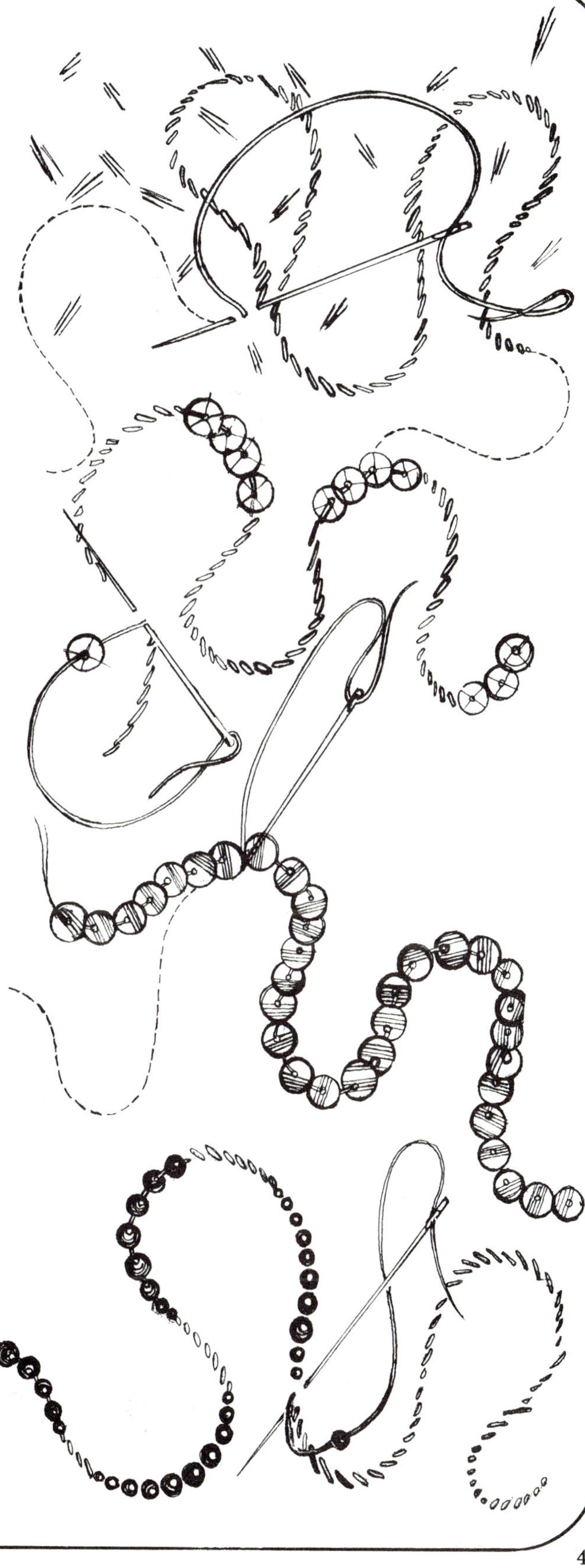

# *Ribbon embroidery*

Have you ever thought of embroidery with ribbon? It is a delightful traditional idea which can be put to a multiplicity of uses in fashion today.

A century ago most ribbon work was highly complicated and demanded meticulous attention to detail. The Victorians had the advantage of a great assortment of ribbons in textures, colours and widths which enabled them to carry out lovely design schemes. Even with our limited range of ribbons it is still possible to invent pretty versions of ribbon embroidery, ranging from straightforward slot-through patterning to the extremely elaborate branch, spray and sprig flower patterns.

In ribbon work it is easy to imitate nature. The simple charm of flowers, fruits and insects can be copied very easily with the added embellishment, if you choose, of ordinary embroidery stitches for minutely detailed work. This type of design is best worked on medium weight linens or loosely-woven woollen materials, for the large-eyed needle will slot with ease between the warp and weft threads leaving the fabric undamaged and it is relatively easy to count the threads over which you are

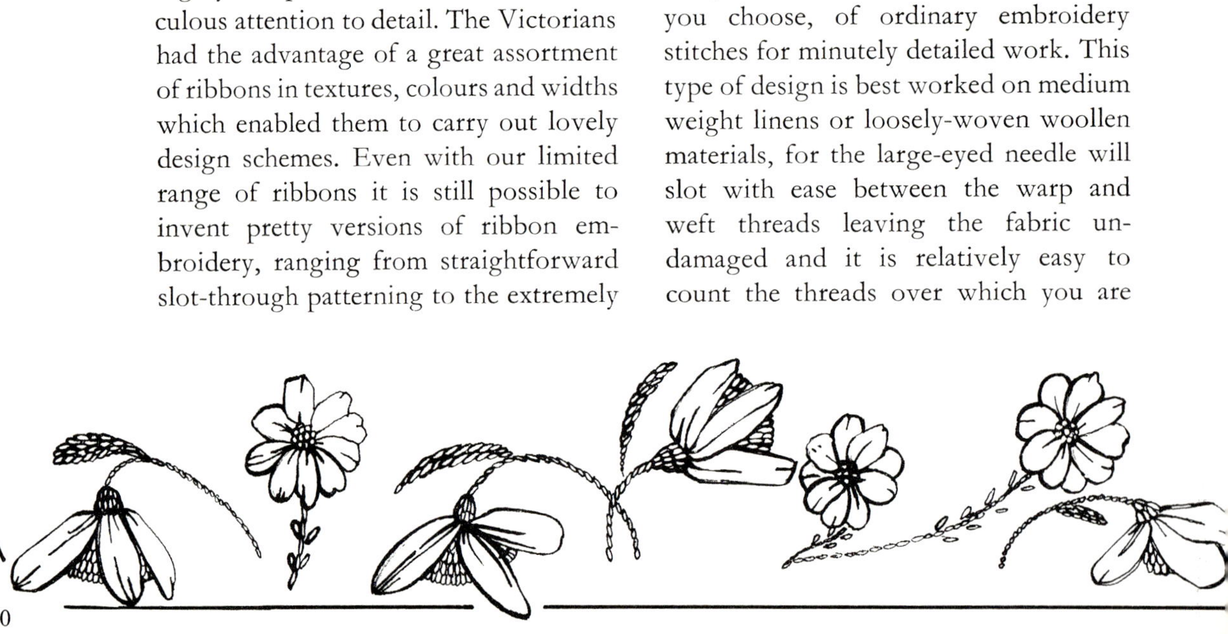

working. Other interesting novelty fabrics can be used to great advantage – try a sprig design in ribbon on a soft angora sweater, a border of daisies and snowdrops down the front of a cardigan, or ribbon kisses in an all-over pattern on a crochet dress.

**Clover stitch** (a)

Using a large-eyed needle and an 18 in. (450 mm) length of ¼ in. (6 mm) satin ribbon, bring the needle up through the fabric, make a ribbon stitch ½ in. (12 mm) long, and slot the needle through to the back. Bring the needle up again an ⅛ in. (3 mm) away from the end of the first stitch, and make another stitch ½ in. (12 mm) long, arranging the angle of the stitch attractively, as shown. Making sure that no ribbon is wasted at the back of the work, continue until the flower is complete.

You can use this stitch to make other flower petals by arranging the individual stitches differently. Add decorative embroidery stitches to link the separate elements of your design, as in the drawings on the facing page.

**Wild grass**

Make stitches in a similar way to those described above, but using a narrower ribbon and arranging them differently.

Decorate each grain with spiky embroidery stitches. The reverse side of both the patterns should have a minimal amount of ribbon overlap. Make stems and bows in satin stitch (see page 57).

Ribbon can also be used to make a slotted pattern similar to saddle stitching, zigzag or herringbone stitch. Nowadays there are no rules. Simply try out your idea, and if the effect is pleasing, your efforts will be successful.

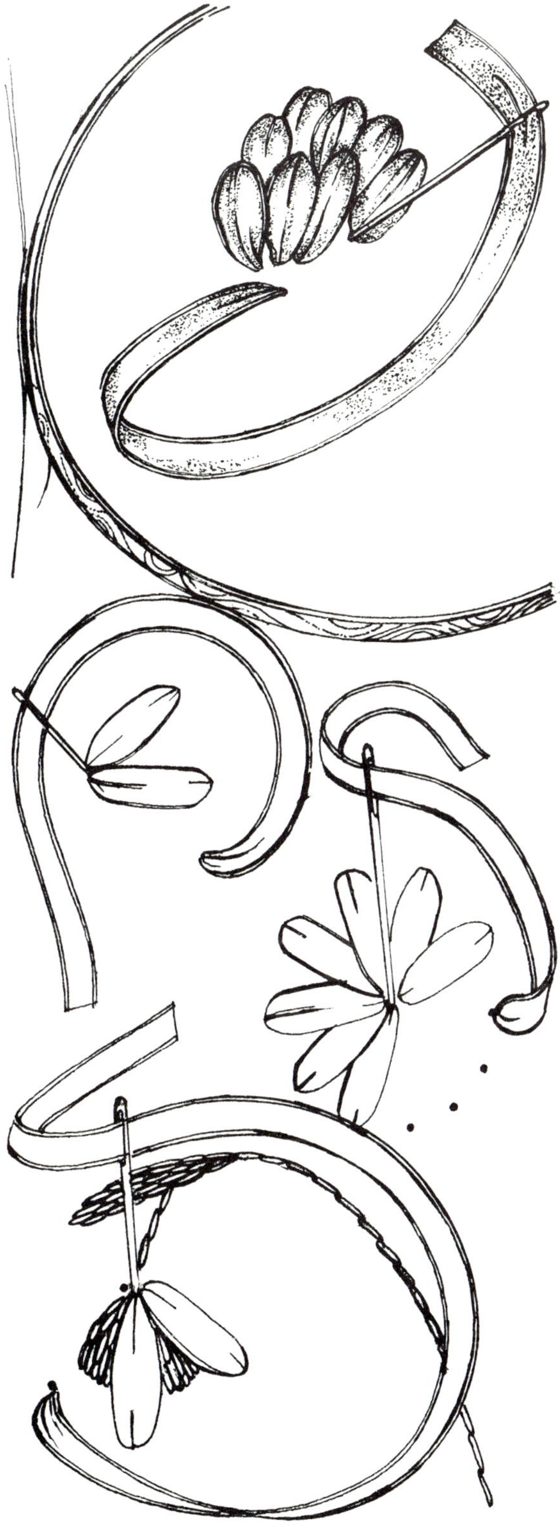

a

# *Chain stitch motif*

You can embroider an exotic pendant motif in vibrant colours and metallic threads using only the simplest of stitches. This one echoes the age of Art

Deco. Embroidered on an evening caftan or a silk tunic worn with velvet pants, it will be strikingly elegant, evoking the splendour of the period.

**Reproducing the design**

This motif was actually worn in the twenties. It has been drawn to its original size. Lay a sheet of strong tracing paper over the motif and follow the outlines with a transfer pencil or a pen dipped in tracing ink. Now transfer the tracing to the fabric by laying it face down against the surface of the dress or tunic and pressing with a hot iron. If you do not have the materials for this method, an alternative would be to 'prick out' the design by means of a tracing wheel with very sharp pins, tracing the entire outline on paper. The pattern can then be transferred by means of a 'pouncing pad' dipped into chalk dust and run over the perforations.

**Embroidery**

Choose brilliantly coloured embroidery threads of silk, braid, chenille or wool. Begin by blocking in the solid areas with random filling stitches to form a padded base and then embroider a regular satin stitch over the top. Set the stitches closely together, letting them fan out slightly towards the outer edge. Now work the outlines in chain stitch.

**Tassel**

Complete the motif with a gorgeous tassel (see page 104). You could use a mixture of threads and materials.

With a little ingenuity you can use this motif in several different ways. It will give an individual look to a pull-on hat, beret, scarf or girdle end, a pocket or sleeve.

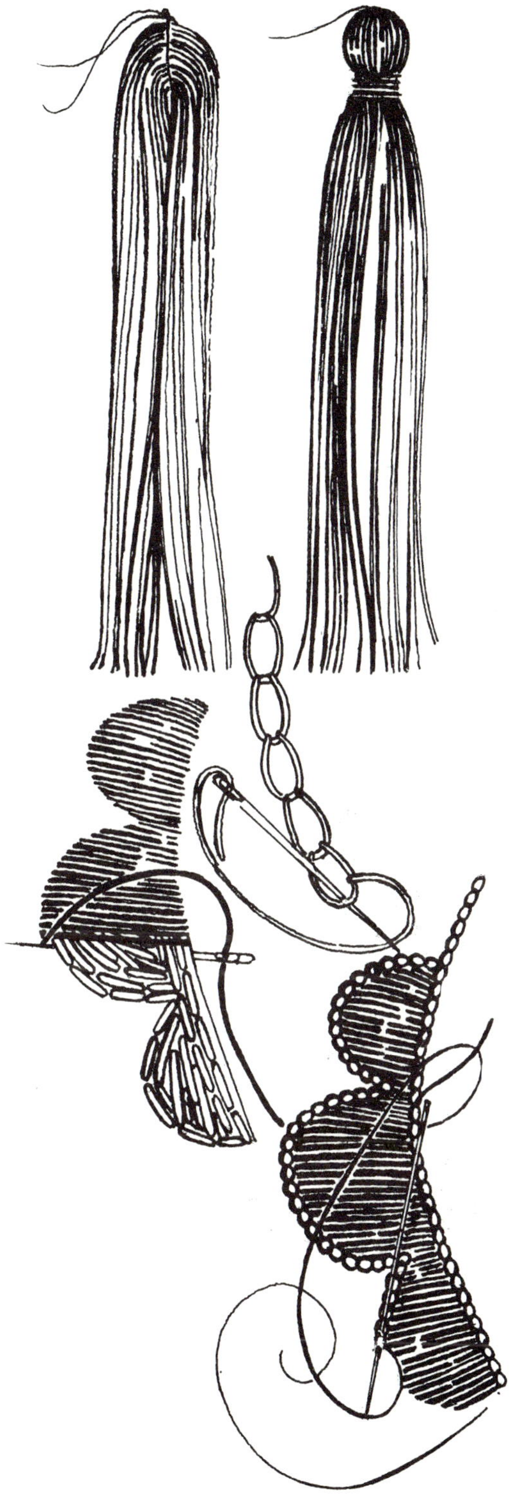

# *Appliqué*

Of all the traditional techniques of decorative sewing, appliqué is the simplest and easiest with which to achieve pretty, exciting and diverse effects. You could decorate a base fabric with a selection of shapes in different colours and textures, or even try pictorial or three-dimensional appliqué.

A plain material can be transformed with an arrangement of several applied motifs – perhaps butterflies in one or two colours on a plain coloured dress. A check gingham dress might have geometric shapes of a different check, or even of the same design turned crosswise against the check of the dress. For impact, nothing beats a bold contrasting appliqué motif designed as the focal point of a dress. Shadowy effects can be achieved with sheers, and georgette shapes applied to the same fabric make a perfect exercise in monotone.

Appliqué is easy. Let your imagination and taste guide you, confident that the result will be in keeping with today's fashion feeling.

### Planning your appliqué

Try out your appliqué ideas by cutting trial shapes in paper, or even in fabric if colour is an important part of the scheme. Pin these into position on the garment, experimenting with changes of shape and position until you are satisfied with the results. Mark the position of each section on the fabric with HB pencil or tailor's chalk.

### Applying motifs of frayable fabric

Mark the outlines of the motifs clearly and cut them out very roughly, leaving a large margin all round. Using your automatic sewing machine apply the motif to the fabric with close satin stitch, and cut away the surplus fabric (a).

### Applying motifs of non-frayable fabric

First stitch the shapes in position by hand or machine, and then decorate them with various embroidered edges – satin stitch, herringbone stitch (b), chain stitch (c), blanket stitch (d), or couching (e).

### Turned-edge technique

Cut out the motifs, leaving a small seam all round. Press the seam allowance under and stitch the shapes in position by hand or machine. For more intricate motifs, cut out the exact shape in stiff paper, then cut the fabric $\frac{1}{4}$ in. (6 mm) larger all round. Lay the paper on the reverse of the fabric and cut it $\frac{1}{4}$ in. (6 mm) larger all round. Turn the edges over the paper and crease them flat with a warm iron. Now remove the paper and slip stitch or topstitch the motif into position. Decorate it with areas of stitchery, beads or braids. (See page 23 for lace appliqué.)

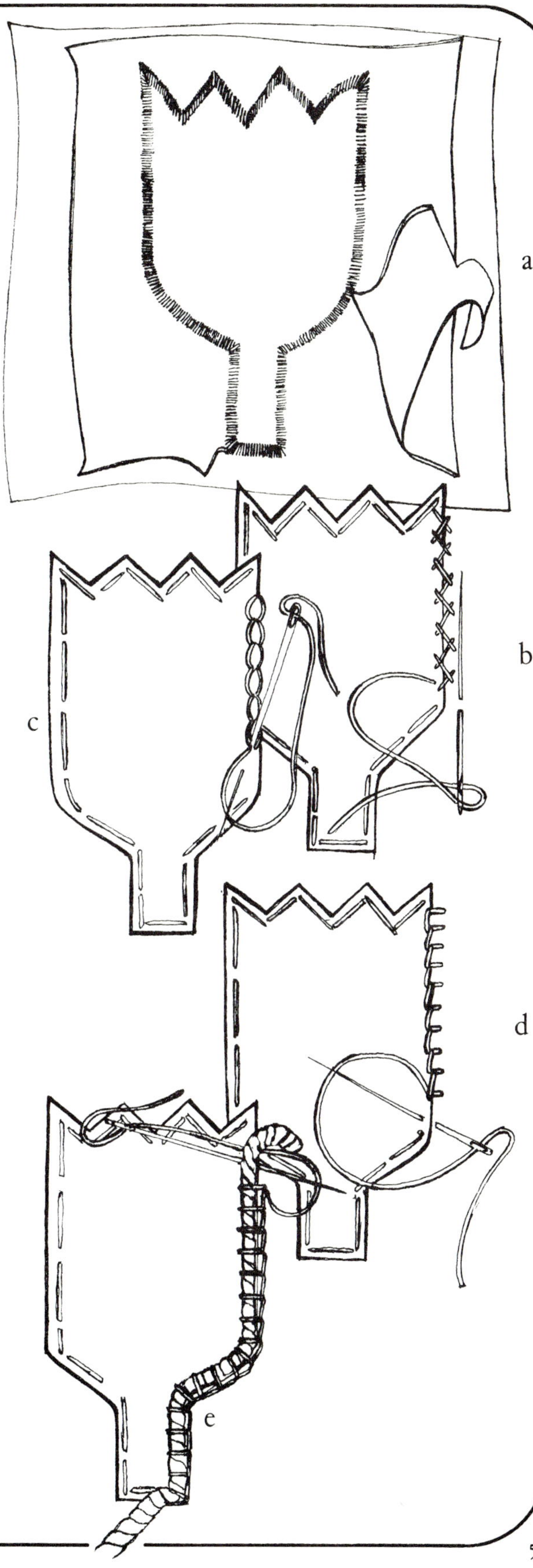

# *Embroidered butterfly*

Gaily coloured butterflies, dragonflies, bees and even bluebirds were once favourite fashion motifs. They are best worked in traditional long and short stitches which lend themselves to perfect colour graduation, as one stitch blends naturally into the next. Vivid, multi-coloured butterflies are so easy to embroider that no-one need be nervous of trying them out. Make them as colourful as the real thing, using their natural shapes and differing sizes to advantage. Work them on a yoke, or apply them as separate motifs on pockets.

**Basic embroidery stitches**

If you are not already skilled in embroidery, study the diagrams to see how easy the stitches are to make. For stem stitch (a) bring the thread through from the back on the lower left hand side of the design and make a diagonal stitch as shown. Continue this, working from left to right, until you have completely outlined the shape required. The antennae may be worked in a slightly smaller, more condensed version of the same stitch (b), also working from left to right. Other diagrams show satin stitch (c), graduated spots in satin stitch (d), long and short stitch (e), and filling stitches which you can use for padding the satin stitch. Try to make all stitches evenly and accurately.

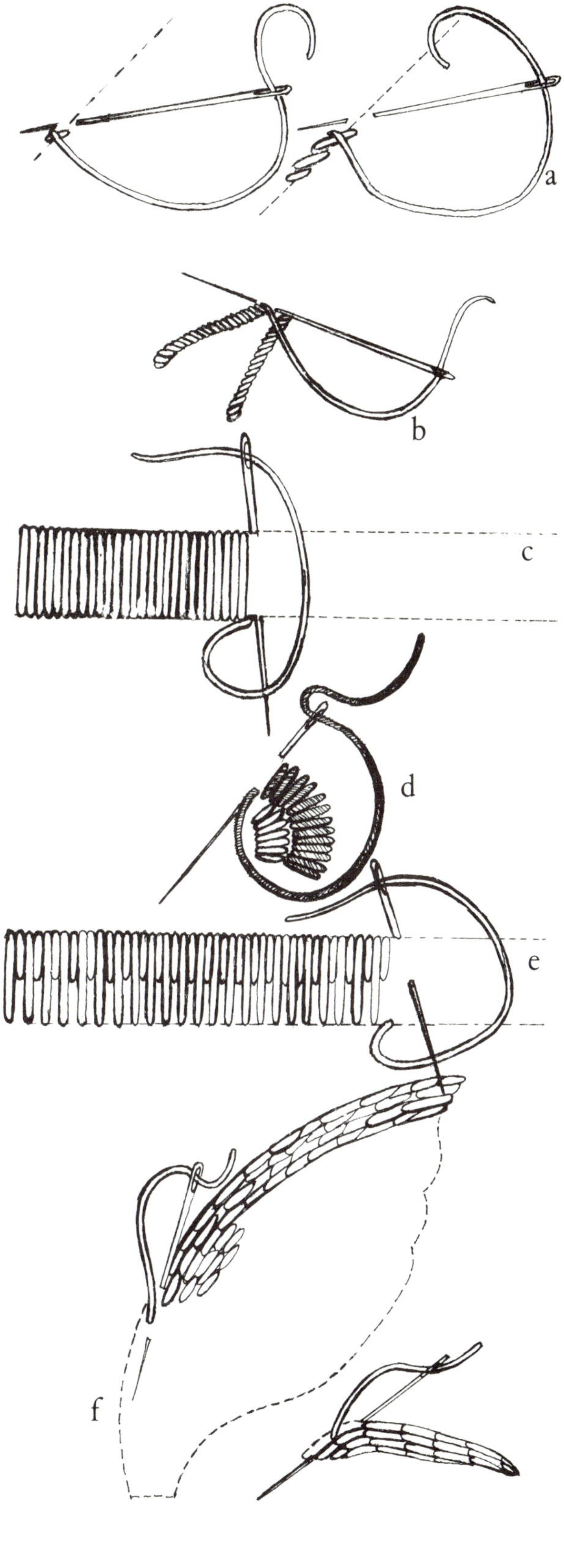


**Making a motif**

Choose three, four or more colours of embroidery silks that blend with each other and relate to or contrast with the colour of the garment. Draw or trace the butterfly shape on to a fairly stiff woven fabric such as tarlatan or fine leno, and then stretch it into an embroidery frame.

First work the spots or other markings in long and short stitches or graduated satin stitch, using stem stitch for the wing veinings. Fill in with long and short stitch between the markings and the wing veining, directing all stitches from the edges towards the body. For the body, use long and short stitches lengthwise. Continue these stitches for the head and add several small stitches in bright colours for the eyes. Leave the antennae until later. Trim the leno to $\frac{1}{4}$ in. (6 mm) all round the motif, turn in the edges and baste them flat. The motif is now ready to stitch to the garment with whipping or running stitch. Now make fine lines of stem-stitching for the antennae and top them if you wish with several parallel satin stitches.

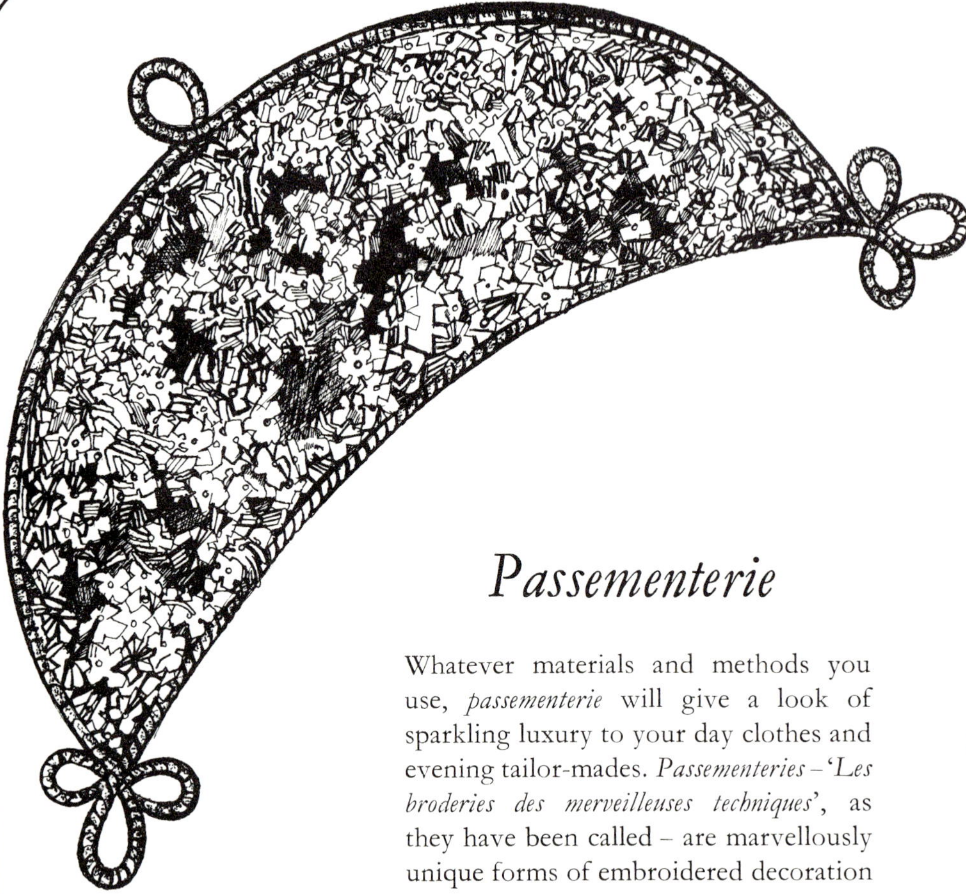

# *Passementerie*

Whatever materials and methods you use, *passementerie* will give a look of sparkling luxury to your day clothes and evening tailor-mades. *Passementeries* – '*Les broderies des merveilleuses techniques*', as they have been called – are marvellously unique forms of embroidered decoration

combining several different techniques and materials. They originated in France and were used with astounding effect by Schiaparelli in the late thirties. Use one to accentuate the high throat of a dress, the importance of a hip, or the drama of an encrusted neckline. Remember that these embroideries must be worn alone, set off by a simple well-cut dress.

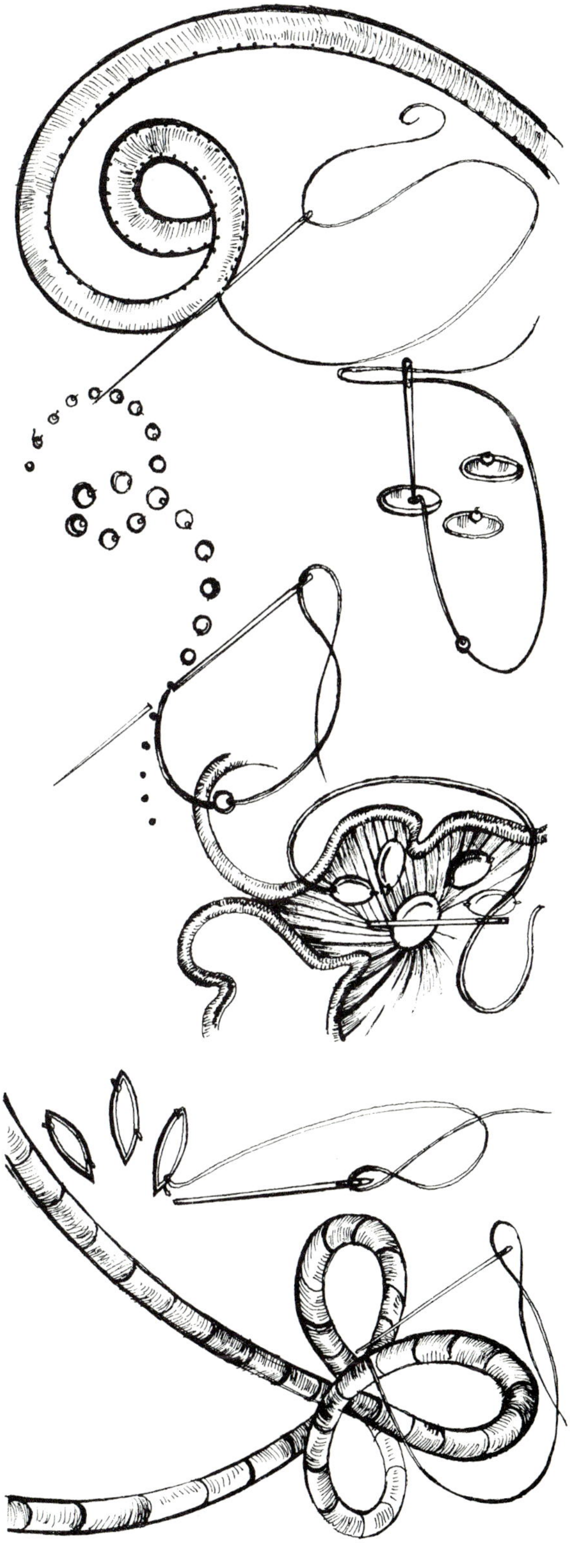

**Outlining the shape**

*Passementerie* may be worked on a separate piece of matching fabric, on a fabric of contrasting texture, or on a lace motif base backed with leno or tarlatan. Experiment first with paper shapes, then mark the outline on the embroidery fabric. Machine stitch the outline before slipping the fabric into a frame.

**Working the passementerie**

First stitch on any textured fabric shapes you fancy. Then couch or slip stitch any braids or cords into position (for couching see page 16). Before completing the design, experiment with arrangements of threads, beads or sequins, and mark them on the paper shape as a guide. You may choose to add sections of long and short stitch (see page 57), metallic outline stitches, beads and sequins (page 68), paillettes (page 72) or leathers, stones or jewels of all kinds. When the design is complete, remove it from the frame and cut the *passementerie* from the base fabric leaving a small edge. Crease back the edges and finish them with close whip stitches.

Instead of doing all the work by hand, you could begin with a patterned base produced by automatic stitchery with a modern machine. Then add fabric shapes, braids, cords and other decorations as you wish.

# *Patches*

Patches are both fashionable and functional. They are the simplest and most convenient way of strengthening points of strain – the heads of pleats, tops of splits and corners of pockets. They not only give reinforcement, but can also add a splash of colour, accentuate cut, and give a stylish look to tailored clothes. You can make a feature of them on points of wear and tear such as knees and elbows, use them to give new life to a tired-looking raincoat, or to pretty up a rather workaday look.

Patches can be made out of a wide range of fabrics from matching shiny plastics, matt suèdes and felts, to prints and companion fabrics used in contrast. They can be repeated elsewhere in the design – on pockets, under collars, inside pleats or as facings.

**Non-frayable fabrics**

Patches in shiny plastics, suèdes, felt and other non-frayable fabrics can be cut with plain or fancy edges. If you want to make a patch with pinked edges in a cotton print you can do so, provided the fabric is firm, by first ironing it on to a Stayflex or similar stick-on cotton backing before cutting it out. Now topstitch round the edges and reinforce each patch by stitching across it from corner to corner.

**Frayable fabrics**

Patches of wool or cotton fabrics must have all their edges turned in before they are stitched in position. Wool will sometimes stretch, so make a trial patch first. Cut out the patches accurately, including seam allowances. Cut corresponding backings of Stayflex or a similar cotton iron-on material without seam allowances. Iron the backings to the wrong side of the patches. Turn in and press down all the edges. Lay the patches in position and pin them flat. Place patches on a new garment before joining the seams. Now, making sure the patches are absolutely correct, machine stitch them in position, slightly overlapping the stitches to finish. Draw the threads through to the back, knot them and press. If you wish, you can decorate the patches with diagonal or horizontal lines of stitching. This method, carefully followed, will ensure a crisp clean patch.

# *Motifs in relief*

The use of hand stitched quilting as a fashion feature has been greatly neglected for years. Now, with the revival of old techniques and the availability of softer and more subtle fabrics, this form of decoration is ready to come into its own again. Quilting was fashionable in the twenties and thirties, when it was continually featured in the Parisian couture collections and contemporary fashion magazines and many inventive adaptations were incorporated into small fashion garments of all kinds.

Snowflakes, circles, squares, lozenges, daisies – all these simple shapes are ideally suitable for padded quilted motifs, and any one of them will add quality and individuality to the look of your garment. Use them differently to produce a variety of effects. Scatter daisies at random over a tunic to add an air of lightness and delicacy. By contrast, lend bulk and weight to a whole area by crowding quilted daisies together throwing the surface into relief so that it resembles a matelassé fabric. Add a formal arrangement of a bunch of daisies to a blouse or tunic to give it a distinctive focal point.

Evoke a different mood by working the open fan design above right – a typical touch of glamour from the thirties. It can look stunning worked in satin, and a satin fan motif applied to a matt finish surface such as taffeta will give a pleasing contrast.

## Quilted daisy

Cut a template in two parts. First draw the outer daisy shape, indicating where the petals come, and cut it out. Make a second template of one petal shape, and then use the two templates in conjunction.

Make the daisy on the fabric before you assemble the garment. Lay the paper pattern piece on the fabric and cut out a larger piece of fabric than indicated. Cut a matching piece of lining, tack it firmly to the fabric, and mark the daisy on it. Starting $\frac{1}{4}$ in. (6 mm) from the outer curve of each one, run stitch the two fabrics together along the straight sides and inner curves of the individual petals. Cut sections of wadding fractionally smaller than the petal template and slot each one into position with the aid of a bodkin before completing the stitching.

## Fan shape

Make a template and cut and tack the fabric and lining pieces as described above. Stitch along the straight outside edges of the fan. Cut the fan-shaped piece of wadding. Stitch through all thicknesses along the radiating vein lines before stitching the outer curves.

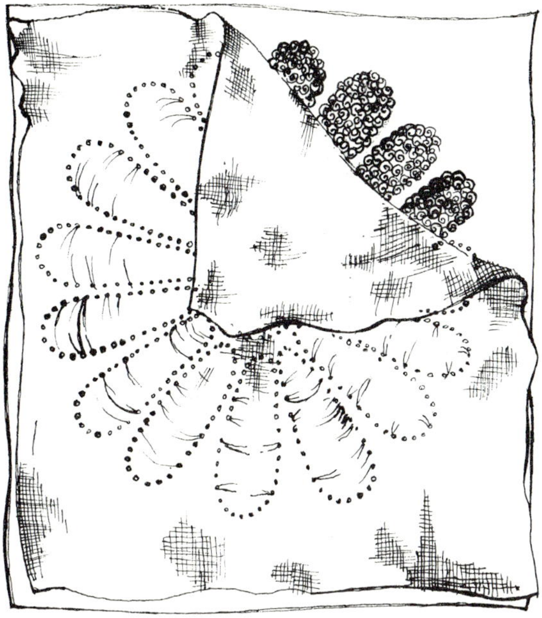

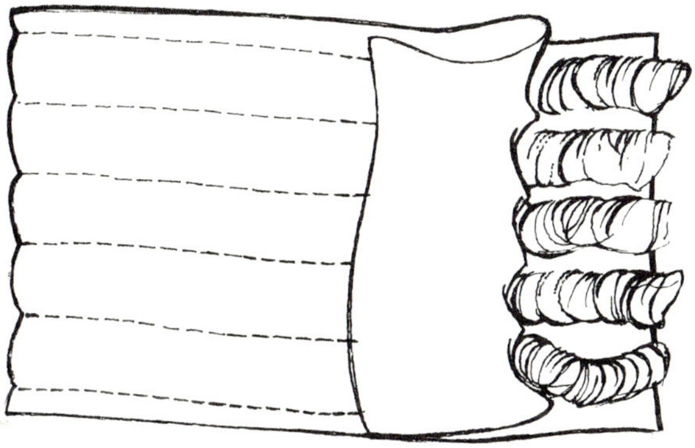

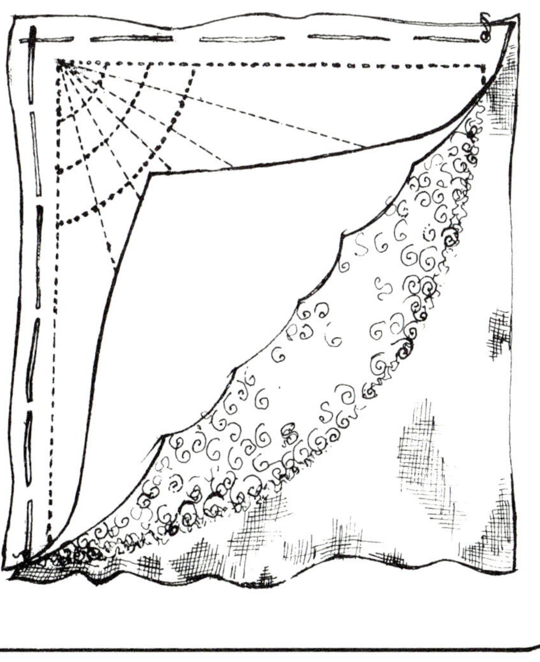

## *Quilting*

For both warmth and drama, quilting is an ideal alternative to fur on collars, cuffs and partial linings. In broad bands it lends weight as a border to coat and sleeve hems, especially when the coat is of a light fabric, and decorative quilting on sleeveless jackets and waistcoats adds extra warmth as well as a touch of fashion.

Designers have invented many novel forms of quilting – embossed patterns in high relief, light and pretty as an eiderdown; pronounced pattern traceries in contrast stitching, sharply outlined to define the pattern on yokes, sleeves and collars; and quilting on printed motifs.

## Materials for quilting

The secret of success is careful planning and preparation, and lavish tacking. Light fabrics should be mounted on a close woven fabric, backed with a layer of fine flannel, then padded with wadding between the mounting and backing. Heavier fabrics should be backed but not mounted.

## Stitching

The most successful stitch is traditional running stitch, although chain embroidery can also be used. Some modern sewing machines have a pressure foot and guide attachments for quilting which prevent drag by the needle, but if your machine does not have the proper attachment it would be best to sew the quilting by hand.

Tack the lining, padding, backing and fabric together in horizontal, vertical and diagonal lines. Using white chalk only, mark the design on to the surface, and stitch.

When making a garment, quilt a large section of fabric before cutting out the pattern pieces. You may like to finish a quilted waistcoat by sewing on tiny beads or buttons where the lines of quilting cross.

Instead of quilting a large area you could try puff-padding a pattern of motifs. Draw motifs on the lining in pencil and stitch the centre of the pattern from the front through fabric and lining. Poke in a puff of wadding to surround the motif. Ease the top fabric to the amount of 'raise' required, then tack round the edges of the wadding, following the pencil line on the back exactly. Again, be sure to finish the quilting before cutting out pattern pieces.

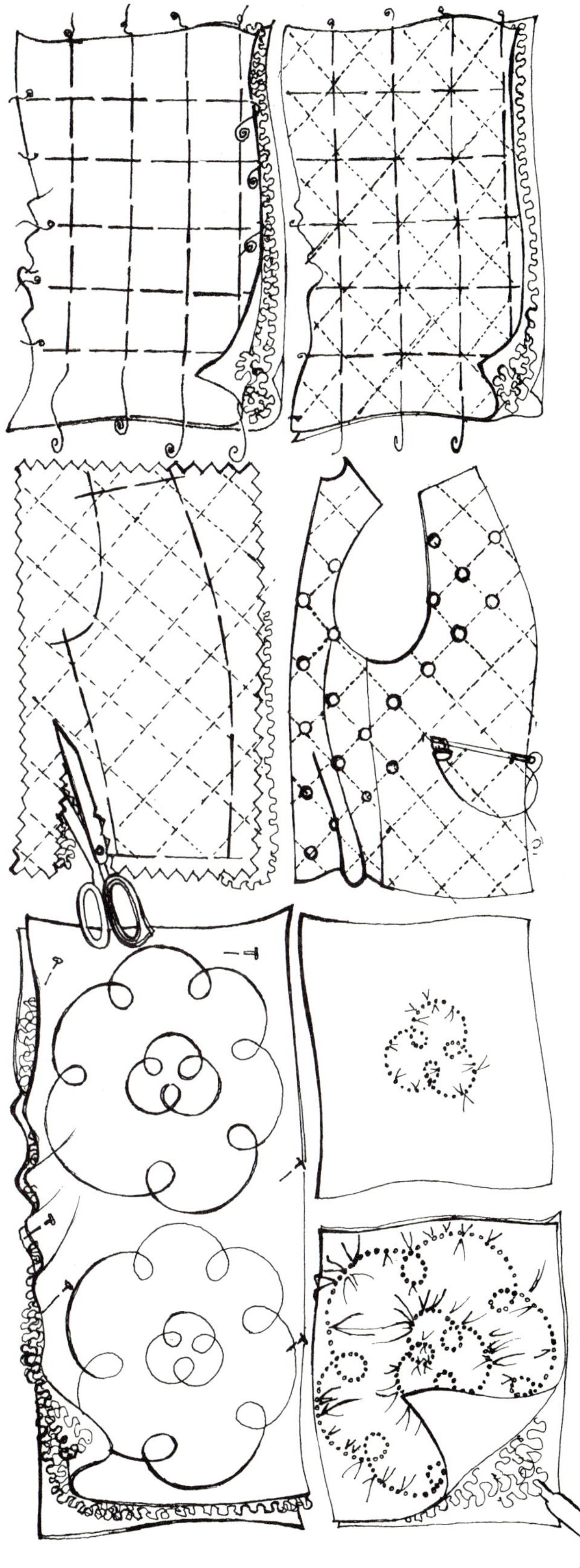

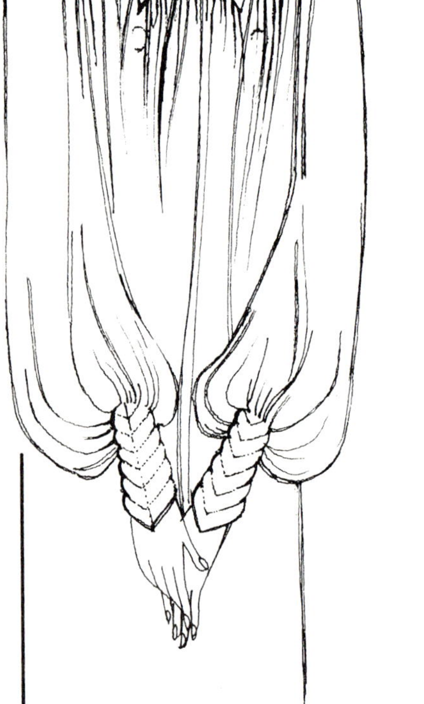

# *Italian quilting*

Patterns both beautiful and decisive can be created in Italian quilting. See how effective these garments are – the dress with cobweb yoke and cuffs, the draped blouse in lingerie satin with single leaf motifs round the neck, and the taffeta jacket embroidered all over with a pattern of scrolled leaves.

The origins of this type of embroidery are deeply rooted in antiquity; it is indigenous to both eastern and Mediterranean countries, and the Italians named it 'Trapunto'. Characteristic designs are plants, spirals and scrolled patterns that meander all over the material. Strands of thick soft wool are threaded through

a channel formed by close parallel lines of stitching in a double thickness of cloth. On opaque fabric a raised corded effect is produced, the padding remaining invisible. On light sheer fabrics such as organza, the look can be transformed by threading brilliantly coloured wools through the design, which will show through in delicate pastel colours. This is known as shadow quilting.

**First attempts at quilting**

Mark the design with double lines on a muslin or similar lining. Tack it securely to the wrong side of the fabric. Then make small running stitches along all the lines of tracery through both layers of fabric. When the design is completely finished, take a large-eyed bodkin and thread strands of wool through from the back. If only part of a garment is to be decorated, do not cut out the dress pattern shape until the quilting is completed. Lay the paper pattern on the fabric and cut pieces of fabric and lining larger than the pattern so as to allow for shrinkage which will be taken up by the quilting. When the quilting is finished, cut out the pattern shape accurately.

Difficulties can arise if a border is to be continuous around a sleeve or hem, or if an all-over pattern is wanted on the body of the garment, because the pattern will probably be interrupted by a seam. If the seam does not come at a focal point, you can ignore it. If that is not the case, however, finish the embroidery a little way away from the seam line. Join the seam, press it open, and then complete the remaining embroidery.

# *Sequins*

Rows and rows of sequins make the simplest and most impressive decoration possible, in broad or narrow bands of gleaming colours, in silver, gold and bronze, or in iridescent mother-of-pearl. Heavy sequined borders are the ultimate in glamour, and make a simple bold trim on a tailored day dress or evening clothes. They can also be twisted into military style designs to add a softening touch to an otherwise severe garment.

For a more delicate effect, light up the edges of your jackets and dresses with just a single strand of sequins. Pick out seams or highlight interesting cutting details on collars, cuffs and pockets on either very dark or white materials. Work sequin strands in all-over designs, trellis border decorations and straight or wavy lines.

In bolder mood, try a garish sequin motif on a plain outfit. Motifs can be bought ready made, but why not design your own for that extra touch of individuality?

### Stitching small groupings of sequins

Spot-mark the required position of each group of sequins with an HB pencil. Use a fine needle and colourless nylon threads or mercerized cotton to match the sequins. Bring the needle up through one of the spots. Thread a sequin on to the needle, oversew it once or twice and finish off securely at the back.

### Applying a line of single sequins

Bring the needle through the fabric and through the first sequin, make a back stitch, and progress forward, catching the next sequin on the needle with the next stitch. Continue in back stitch, adding more sequins as you go.

### Applying sequin strips

Run stitch, slip stitch or couch (see page 17) over the thread between every fifth sequin. When applying bands of multiple rows of sequins, pin the band securely in position before couch stitching across the sequin thread at every fifth sequin.

### Making a motif

Arrange the sequins on a piece of stiffened muslin or leno held in an embroidery frame before stitching them in position. You can combine the sequins with beads and cords as for *passementerie* (see page 58).

### Applying a motif

Pin the motif in position on the garment and hand stitch around the edge, using either a blanket stitch or side stitch. Attach the motif to the fabric through the centre if necessary.

# *Diamanté*

Diamanté has adorned dresses and enriched embroideries for years, and the appeal of this form of imitation diamond is still with us.

Scatter sheer fabrics all over with stars, or buy diamanté in single strands or double and triple braids to outline an edge. Give a clinging evening dress an instant thirties look with glittering shoulder straps; or draw attention to a slim waist with swinging diamanté tassels that swish as you walk.

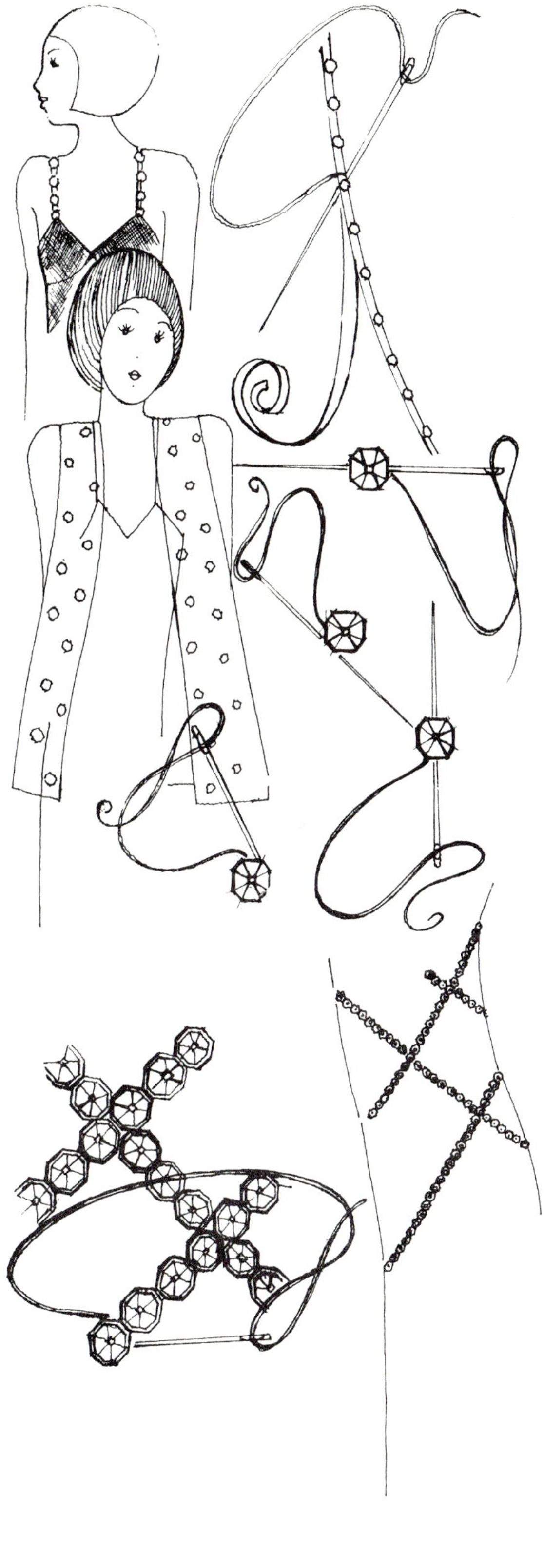

**Attaching single diamantés**

Single diamantés with a clear or tinted finish can be bought by the dozen. First prepare your surface by marking the position of each diamanté with a sharp HB pencil. Using a fine needle and matching thread, bring the needle up from the inside of the garment to the spot where the diamanté is to be. Pass the needle from right to left, through the centre hole of the diamanté, and then stitch $\frac{1}{8}$ in. (3 mm) away from the point where the thread emerges. Bring the needle up again at the bottom edge of the diamanté and pass the needle through the second hole from bottom to top. Take the needle through to the back and tie the loose ends without pulling.

**Attaching a strip of diamanté**

Start with the needle tip to the right of the first diamanté on the strip. Pass the thread over the first diamanté and back through the material $\frac{1}{8}$ in. (3 mm) to the side. Repeat this stitch to make it firm. Next, bring the needle through to the right of the fourth diamanté along the strip and repeat the same stitch. Continue with evenly spaced stitches along the strip.

**Shoulder straps**

Use the couching method to stitch a diamanté strip to a tape, fabric rouleau or velvet ribbon.

# *Paillettes*

Scattered on your evening jacket, paillettes will sparkle like diamonds. Use them as your inclination takes you; the effect will be magical.

Paillettes are small metallic shapes like sequins. They come in many different varieties – gold leaves and moons, silvery stars, multicoloured flowers. Look for them on the trimmings counter in your local department stores, or even in an old-fashioned bead emporium if one still exists in your vicinity. Street markets are a good source too, for you can rob an old dress of its paillettes. Try as many different sources as possible to build up an interesting collection.

You may wish to trim an existing garment, or perhaps one pattern piece of a dress you intend to make yourself. In either case, try tossing paillettes at random all over the material and see what kind of effect you can obtain. You may opt for a random design, or a jewelled spray. Alternatively, use them to emphasize an embroidery pattern, add them to a design of couched Russia braid, or choose two or three shapes to compose into a formal border.

Paillettes look particularly effective as decorations for evening 'cover-up' garments – boleros, jackets, waistcoats, or net shoulder capes worn with long evening skirts or low-cut dresses.

### Stitching on paillettes at random

Attach each shape singly, with nylon thread, either colourless or the same colour as the paillettes or fabric. Take a few firm stitches through the pierced hole over on to your fabric. Secure the thread firmly from behind, taking care not to pull too hard.

A plan is useful even for a random design, but for any sort of formal arrangement it is essential for success.

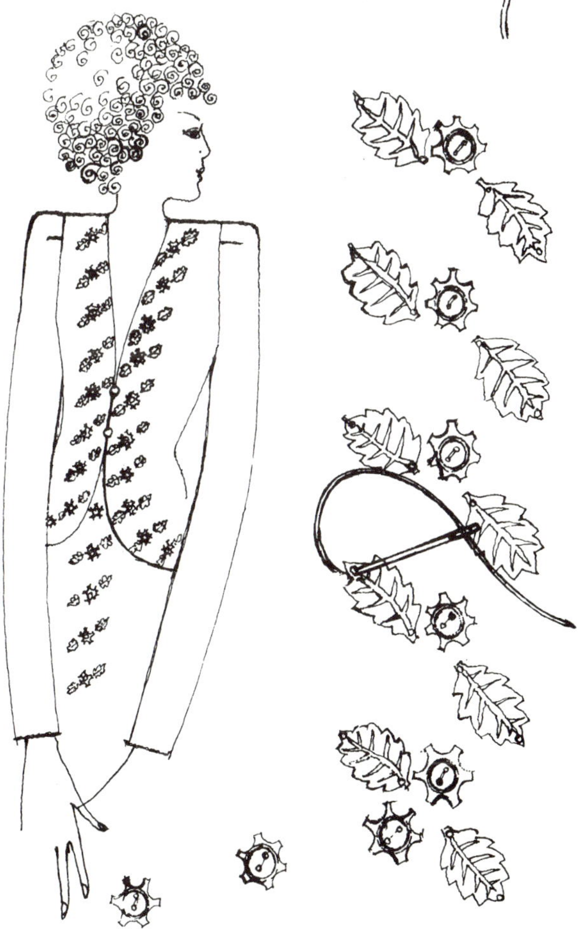

### Paillettes and embroidery in a formal arrangement

Decorate one or more sections of the garment before you make it up. Lay the relevant paper pattern flat. Take your embroidery threads or braid and experiment by twisting and turning them to form a single repeat of a preconceived pattern, adding a paillette here and there to accentuate the design. With a tape measure to hand, work out exactly the correct size and scale of your design, and finally draw it in HB pencil on your paper pattern section. When satisfied with your design, lay a strong sheet of tracing paper over the pencilled pattern and trace out a transfer to reproduce on the material. (Another method of reproducing a design is described on page 53.)

Choose your colours carefully. An embroidered design like the one above right would look delightful worked on oyster satin, using couched-on gold soutache or other thin braid (see page 17) and highlighted with little gold starry paillettes.

# *Beading*

Transparent glass beads in many colourings such as sapphire, topaz and amethyst, are available in a variety of flat shapes and pendant drops. With patience you can embroider simple beaded arrangements to form matching or contrasting braids and strips. These can be stitched to a garment after completion to give sparkling emphasis to a hem or the neck edge of a caftan or tunic. For more formal evening wear, pretty traceries of dangling motifs will give a delicate and at the same time rich effect when carried out in the same colour as the fabric. This treatment is especially effective in pale colours – blondes, pale blues and pinks – and suitable for fabrics such as fine woollens, crêpes, velvets and satins.

**A beaded strip braid**
Cut a trial width of fabric. Select different sizes and shapes of beads and move them about on the fabric, experimenting with repeating patterns. When satisfied with the result, estimate the number of beads and the yardage of braid you will need. Cut a fabric strip to the required width plus seam allowances, and lightly press the entire length flat. Using a sharp HB pencil and tape measure, spot-mark the positions of the beads. Thread a fine needle with transparent synthetic thread and begin stitching the beads in place, concentrating on just one size and type. Take care not to pull the thread too tightly. Now turn to one of the complementary-shaped beads and stitch on all the beads of that type. It is important to keep the beads a sufficient distance from the edge of the braid to allow for the attaching of facings or other sections of the garment.

**Beading a shaped section**
Where a shaped section of a dress is to be beaded, fit and shape it to the correct size, making any darts or tucks. Sew on the beading as described above, finishing it ½ in. (12 mm) away from all edges and seam lines. Finish making up the dress section before completing the beading up to the seams and edges.

**Decorative tracery** (facing page)
Tack-mark the position of the proposed tracery. Thread a fine needle with transparent thread and run stitch or couch the criss-crossed lines of bugle beads to your bodice. Sew on the pendant drops individually afterwards, stitching through the ring inserted at the top of each drop.

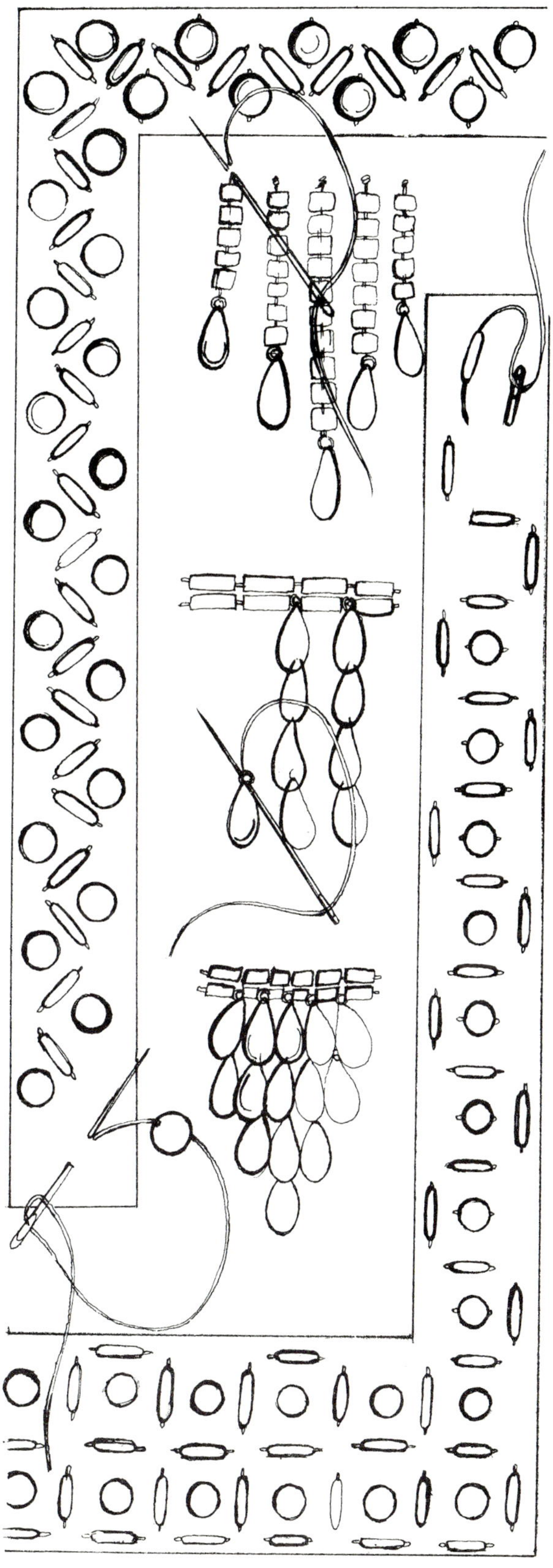

# *Elastication*

While still retaining its practical functions, elastication has become an element of fashion design. Whereas its main function used to be to hold up the bloomers of the modest, designers now use it in a variety of pretty and effective ways to draw in waists, wrists and necklines. Placed strategically in the design and cut of a garment, elastic also gives clothes adaptability for quite a long time.

A favourite way of using elastic is as a drawstring. It can be from ½ in. (12 mm) wide, used either as a single strip or in multiple bands, which add interest to the design while giving extra comfort to the wearer.

Another form of elastication that is both functional and decorative is the new soft elasticated webbing which is ideal for waistbands on skirts, slacks and short jackets.

**Elastication drawstring fashion**
Thread band elastic $\frac{1}{2}$–1 in. (12–25 mm) wide through a series of channels separated by single, double or triple lines of decorative stitching. To make the channels, cut a strip of lining or self fabric the length and width of the area to be elasticated, plus 1 in. (25 mm) seam allowance. Working from the front, pin the strip to the inside of the garment and tack it securely in place. Mark the sewing lines with chalk, making each channel $\frac{1}{8}$ in. (3 mm) wider than the elastic (b) so that it will be drawn through easily. Thread the elastic into the channels and draw it up (c). Machine stitch across the elastic inside the seam allowance for extra security.

**Elasticated webbing**
Webbing bands, obtainable by the yard or metre, can become part of the design of the garment when used on wrists or on the waists of skirts, slacks and jackets. Cut the elastic stretched out to the length required plus seam allowance. Lay it against the edge of the fabric.

Stretch the elastic as you stitch it in place. When folded down, the band will draw the garment into gathers. Finish the seam edges with zigzag stitch on the machine, or whip closely by hand.

**Elasticated shirring**
For elasticated shirring (diagrams a and d) see the shirring section on page 79.

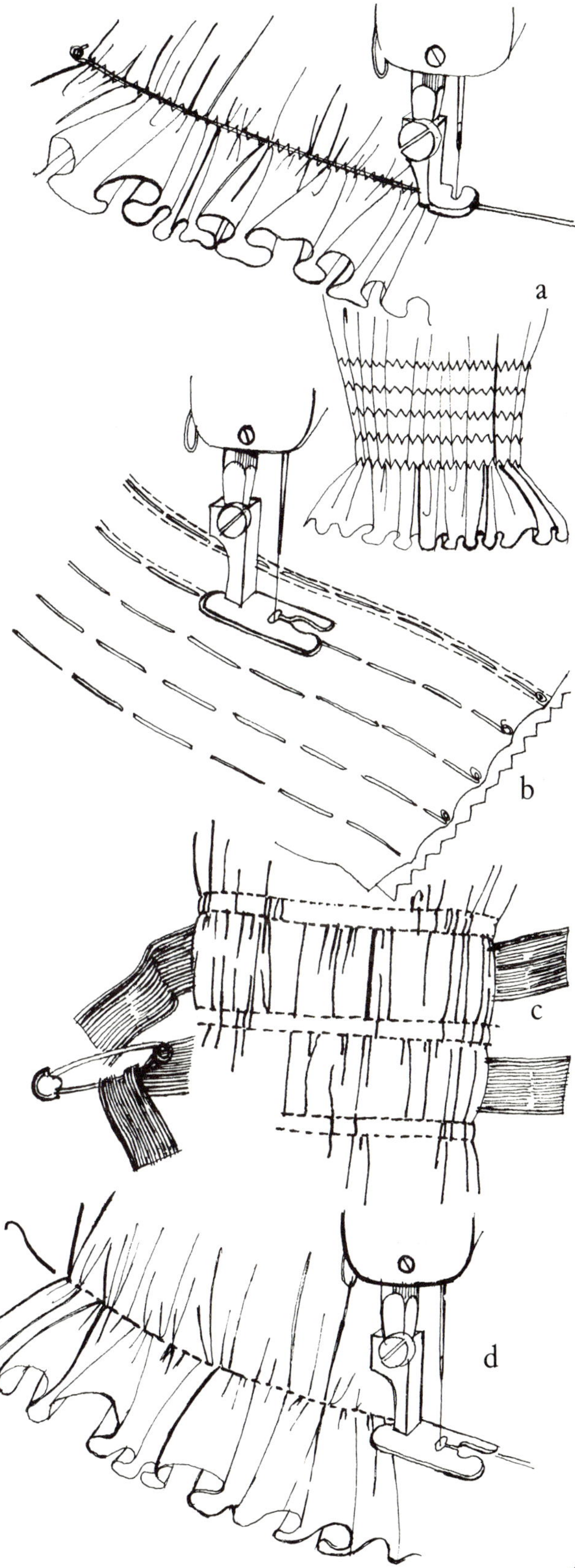

# *Shirring*

Shirring is a functional, adaptable and versatile form of gathering also known as gauging. It can look formal, glamorous or, when combined with frills, edgings and embroideries, prettily feminine.

To decorate shirring, stitch over the rows of gathers by machine, or work over them with outline embroidery stitches. In this case the lines of gauging are used as a basis for imitation smocking, giving a very pretty 'rainbow' effect. For boldness try tucked and corded shirring choosing the weight of the cord according to the effect you need. Elasticated shirring (stitched by machine, with shirring elastic in the bobbin) is a boon when flexibility is needed, as illustrated here in the gypsy dress.

**Simple shirring**

Allow three times the amount of fabric required for the finished measurement. Mark where the shirring will go, either by drawing chalk lines on the fabric or by making use of a notched guide. Where close lines are required, press the machine foot against the previous line of stitching as a guide (c).

Shirring is either evenly run stitched by hand (a), or sewn by machine using a fairly large stitch and a loose tension to allow the loose gathering lines to be drawn up individually from the back. When the fullness has been evenly adjusted, fasten these lines of stitching separately at the back. Decorative forms of stitching can be sewn with an automatic machine.

Sometimes it is necessary to back shirring with a strip of lawn (b) or tapes (e) to help it keep its shape, though very often you will find that back stitching on the reverse is sufficient (d).

### Tucked and corded shirring

Tucked shirring consists of successive rows of narrow gathered tucks (see page 10) drawn up on the stitching line. Corded tucks make an even bolder form of shirring which can be drawn up over narrow cable cords or ropes. First mark the guidelines on your fabric, then lay a cord on each line and fold the material over the cord. Make running stitches through both thicknesses of cloth, as close to the cord as possible (f). Draw up the gathering stitches as you advance pushing the gathers back over the cord, but leaving sufficient thread at the end of each row to make adjustments. Stay one end of this shirring with a row of stitching, to stop the cord disappearing down the tuck when adjustments are made. If preferred, run a cord on a bodkin through the tucks afterwards to give permanent gathers, or substitute the cord with corded elastic for flexibility. This elasticated tucking can also be achieved by some electric machines.

### Elasticated shirring

This is mentioned in the section on elastication (page 77).

Shirring elastic may be attached to the wrong side of a garment with a zigzag machine stitch (diagram (a) page 77) or wound on to the bobbin and stitched in the usual way (b).

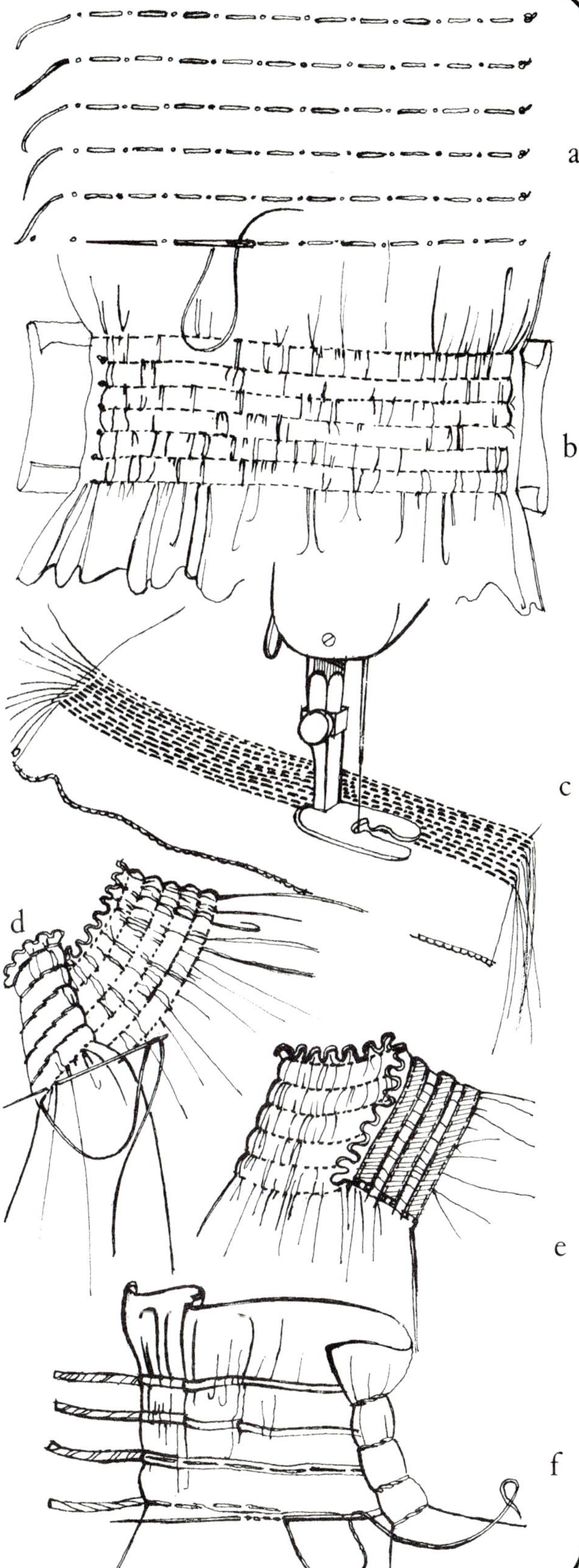

# *Featuring fullness*

Fullness can look pretty or glamorous on an extra special dress. Nestle your head against gigantic puff sleeves in rich rippling velvet; make swagged or draped sleeves in slippery satin or insert blistered bands of gathering into gentle crêpes and shot or shaded taffetas. Try incorporating just one exaggerated idea like this into a starkly cut dress of simple line. Make it of net, crisp paper taffeta or velvet, blancmange-coloured nylon, lamé, crêpe or lingerie satin for a true thirties look.

**Gathered bands**

Draw the width and position of the bands on your paper pattern and cut out the fabric, allowing $\frac{1}{2}$ in. (12 mm) seams in the body of the dress where the bands are to come. Cut the strips for the bands, again allowing $\frac{1}{2}$ in. (12 mm) seams, making them two to three times the desired finished length. Set your machine to a large stitch and loosen the tension. Run a parallel line of loose stitches along each long edge just inside the seam line (a) and draw the gathers up evenly to the required length. Pin the gathered band in position right sides together, and tack and machine stitch in the normal way (b). With the point of the iron, gently flatten the seams, keeping the iron away from the gathered section.

**Puffed sleeves**

Cut two normal sleeves in a fairly stiff lining fabric. These will be the undersleeves. Using your normal sleeve pattern as a guide, cut one larger section in unbleached calico to act as a toile, adding at least 12 in. (300 mm) to the height and 18 in. (450 mm) to the width. Prepare the undersleeve in the normal way and try gathering and arranging the toile over it, trimming it or cutting a second time if necessary. While the experimental toile is pinned in position on the stand, mark the exact edges and indentations and also the balance points of the sleeve head to the armhole. Remove the toile, trim it again if necessary and iron it flat. Use it as a guide for cutting out the sleeves, leaving seam allowances. Make up the sleeves and use the guide marks to fit them into the armholes. Stitch some of the fullness together into neat gathers as necessary (c).

**Draped puff sleeve**

Work as for the ruched puffed sleeves. Arrange the top pleats of the left-hand sleeve, then repeat them exactly on the right-hand sleeve, mirror fashion. Next arrange the left-hand front pleats, repeating again on the right. Then make the back pleats. When both sleeves have been arranged and match exactly, tack and machine stitch the seams together and insert the sleeves in each armhole in the usual way (d).

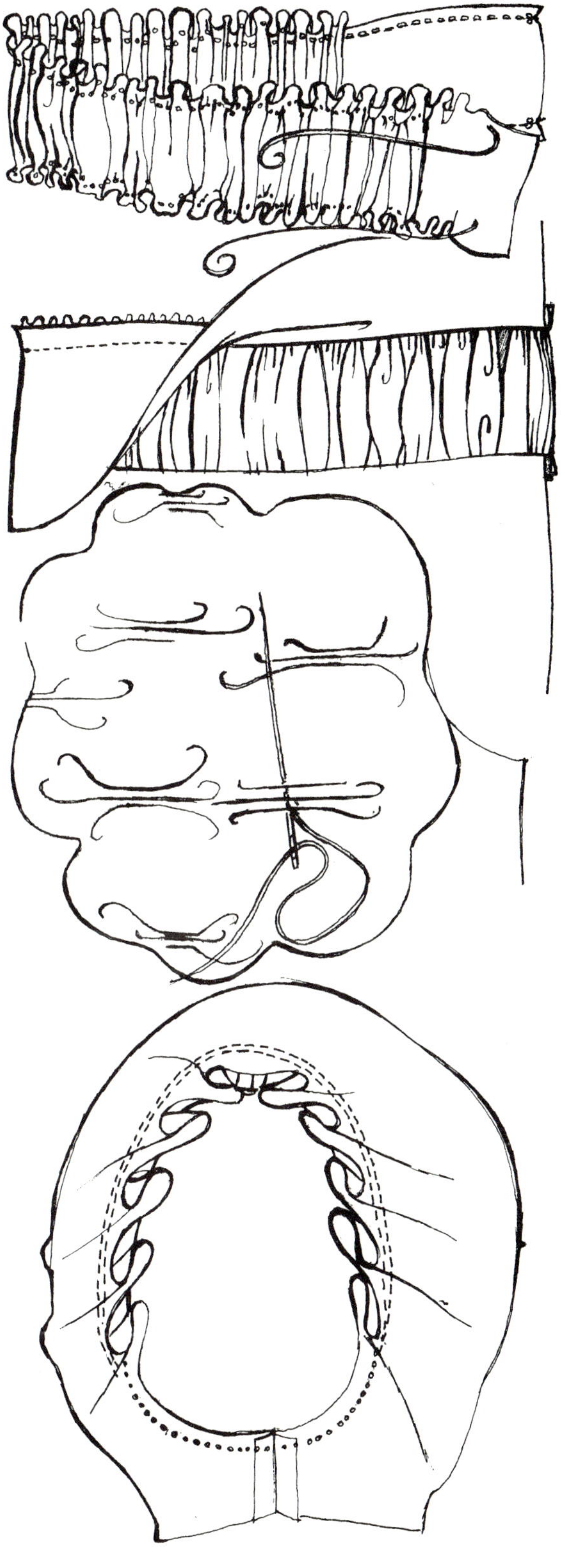

a

b

c

d

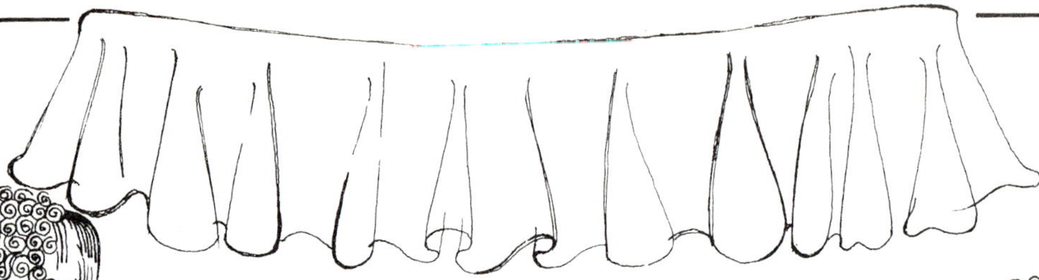

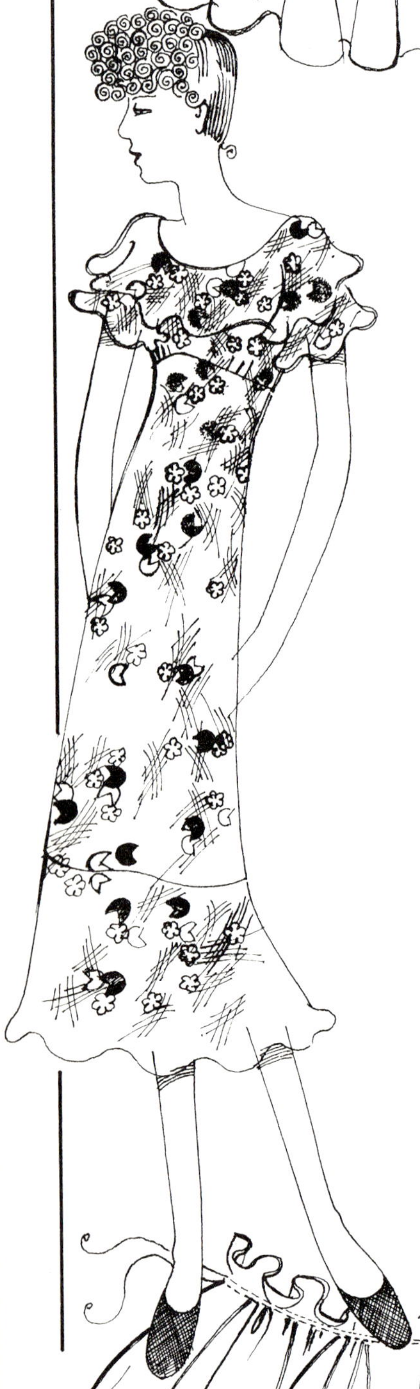

# *Frills and flounces*

Now that fitted waists, high heeled shoes, flowered hats and long dresses can be worn at any time of the day, you can revive to advantage such delightfully feminine trimmings as frills and flounces for day wear as well as evening.

It is important to distinguish between the two, for although they are used in a similar way, they are cut quite differently. A frill is a strip of any desired width of material, cut usually on the straight but sometimes on the cross, and gathered or pleated to the edge of the garment. A flounce is used where the aim is for a more gentle flow. It is cut on a spiral principle, so that a smooth, curved edge is attached to the straight edge of a garment, forming a fluted hem.

**A simple frill**

Use chalk to mark a series of parallel lines on the cross grain of the fabric. The total length of the lines should measure three times the proposed width of the frill. The distance between them should be the depth of the frill plus seam allowances on the top and bottom edges. Cut out the strips and join them into a loop, sewing the seams along the natural grain. Finish the hem by hand, with straight or zigzag machine stitches,

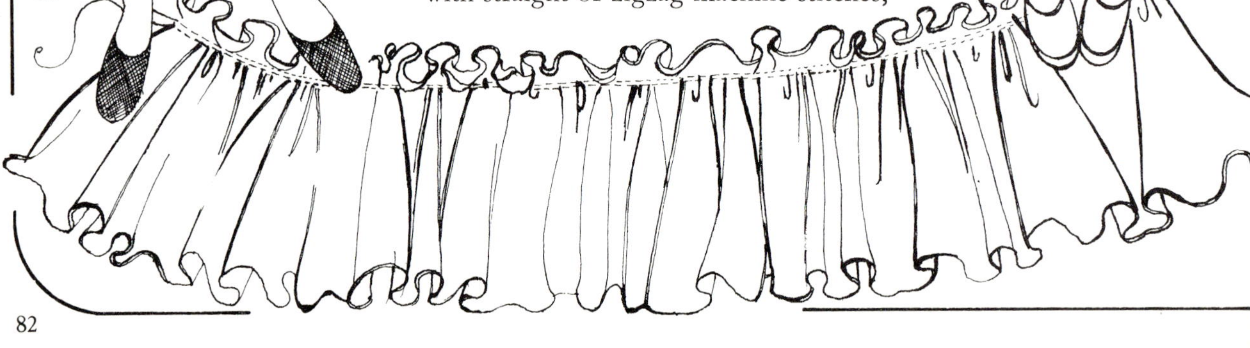

with lace or with a machine embroidered edge of cut scallops. Sew along the top edge of the frill with two parallel lines of large loose machine stitching. Before pulling up the gathers, mark both the frill and the hem into quarters or eighths. Match the marks, draw up the gathers and machine stitch the frill to the garment. If you are attaching the frill to a raw edge, lay frill and garment right sides together before sewing. If attaching it to a hem, sew the frill to the wrong side of the garment (a). Instead of gathering, you could fold the frill into a series of pleats (b).

**Frill with a decorative heading** (c)
To make a heading 1 in. (25 mm) deep, allow an extra $2\frac{1}{2}$ in. (65 mm) to the depth of the frill when marking it out. Turn back the top of the frill $1\frac{1}{2}$ in. (35 mm), press down the edge, and make gathering lines 1 in. (25 mm) from the folded edge. Lay the frill on top of the unfinished raw edge of the garment. Pin securely through three layers and join by topstitching through all thicknesses along either the top or bottom gathered line or, better still, along both lines.

**A flounce**
Cut a square of fabric. Starting at the lower right-hand corner of the square and ignoring the corners, draw a line spiralling in towards the centre (d). When you start on the second round of the spiral, make sure that the distance between the lines is equal to the depth needed for the flounce. Cut along the lines. Finish the outer curved edge as for the bottom of the frill and sew the inner edge to the straight edge of the garment.

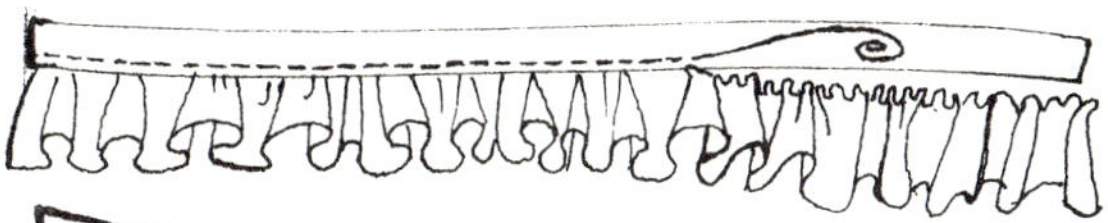
a

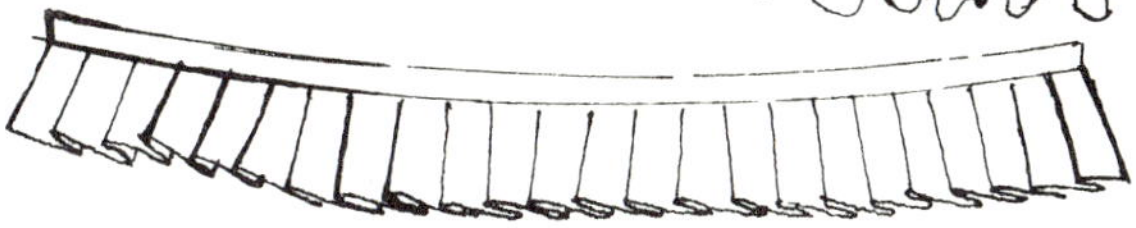
b

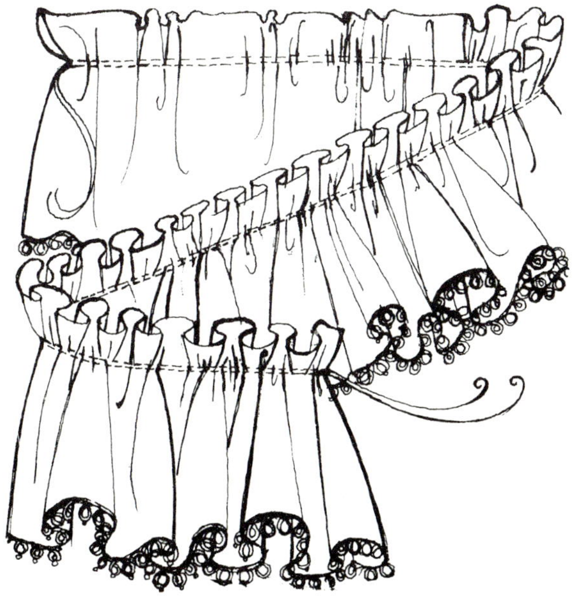
c

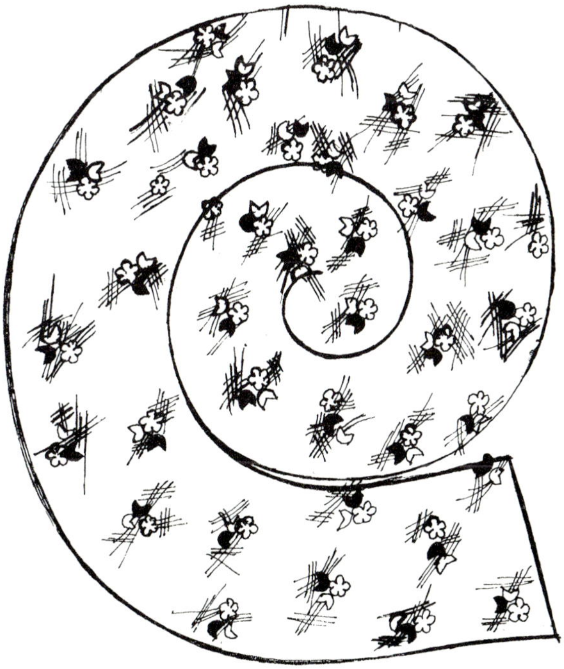
d

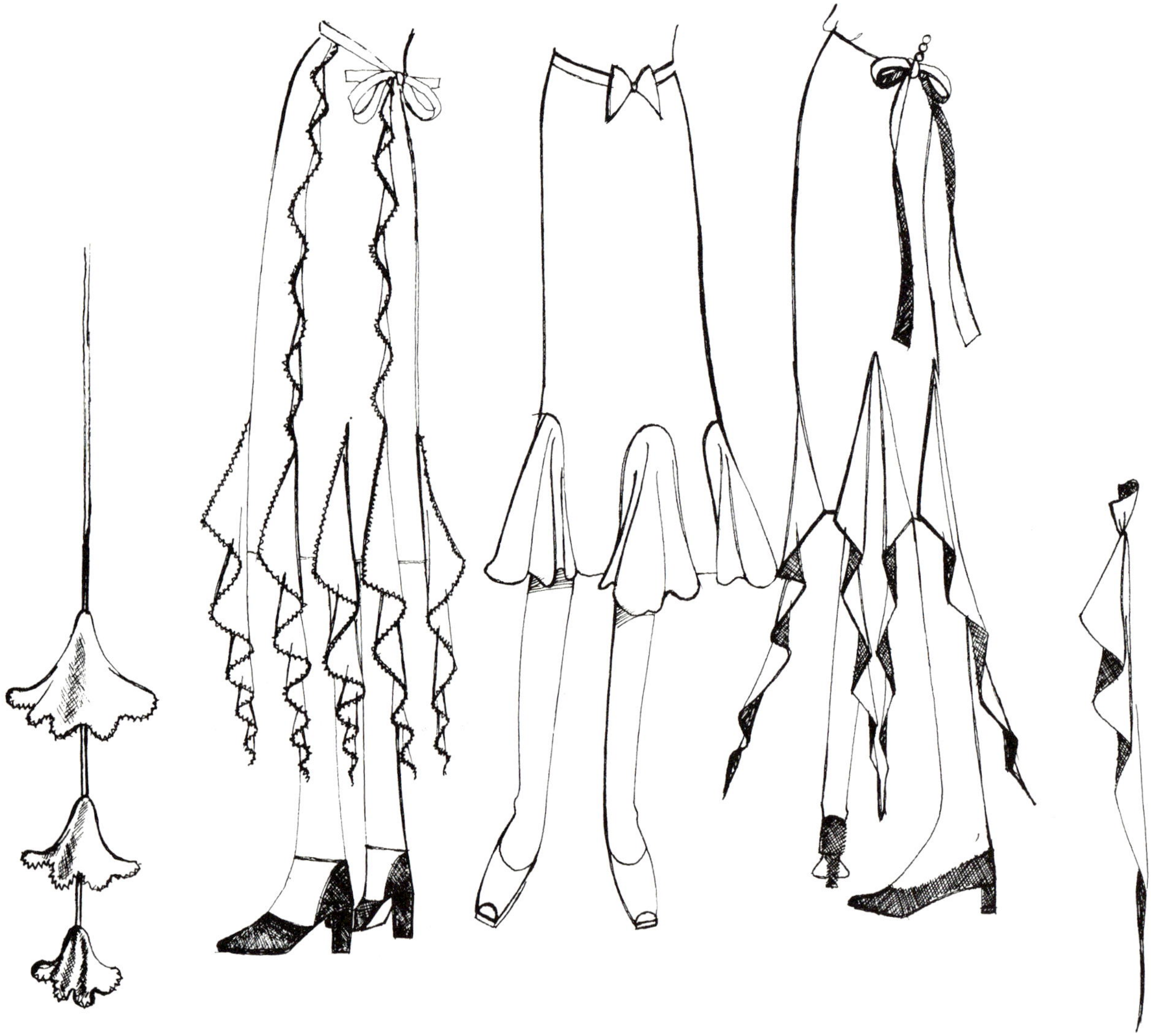

# *Godets and handkerchief points*

Fashion is a matter of contrasts and contradictions. Following fast on the heels of the phenomenon called 'shape' in the late sixties came the 'fluid look', the first sign of a nostalgic harking-back in fashion to which we have now become accustomed. Fluidity, reborn after an absence of well over thirty years, has given us back the bias cut, the godet, the handkerchief point, fishtails and waterfalls, all in the newer, more supple fabrics. It was Madame Vionnet who introduced a fashion revolution in the twenties, inventing a whole new way of bias cutting, together with an intricate new method of making it up. The purpose of the godet – a triangular, flared inset – was to give extra fullness and movement to the dress and it was sometimes allowed to trail in handkerchief points to the ground.

### Curved-top godet

Cut a paper pattern the shape and size of the section desired (dotted line, diagram a) folding the paper pattern in half lengthwise to ensure that it is symmetrical. Lay the pattern on the skirt material and mark its position. Tack round the marks and cut away the section inside them, leaving ½ in. (12 mm) turning. Now cut the godet section to be inset. Using the original curved top cut a new paper pattern, flaring the sides out 3–6 in. (75–150 mm) and keeping the seam lines exactly the same length. Curve the hem and add seam and hem allowances. Cut the godet on the cross grain of the fabric and set it into the skirt. Use the same method for pointed godets.

### Handkerchief points

Make kite-shaped sections (b) and set them into triangular cut-out sections.

### Fishtail

This is a triangular piece of fabric caught vertically along its long end, the rest left hanging freely. It is either cut as a piece of single fabric and finished by hemming or machining, or faced in a contrasting colour.

It is fun to play with circular trimmings, too, using whole, half and quarter circles. Half circles stitched along sleeve seams make an intriguing fan-shaped decoration, while jersey circles, with zigzag edges suspended on a satin rouleau, make an exotic flower finish (c).

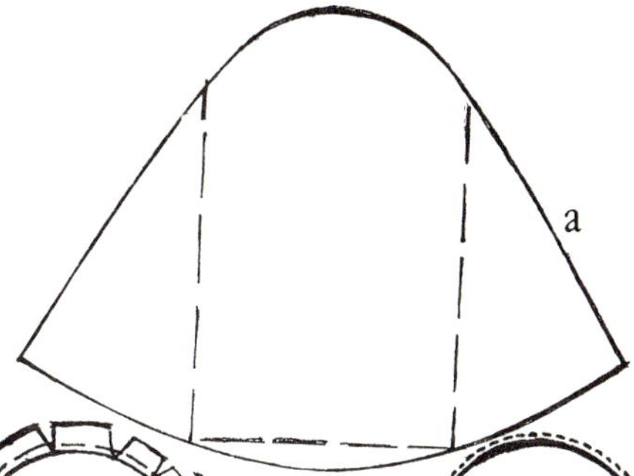

a

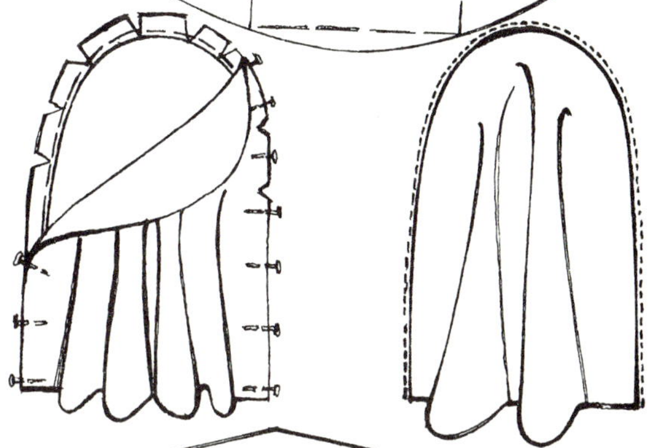

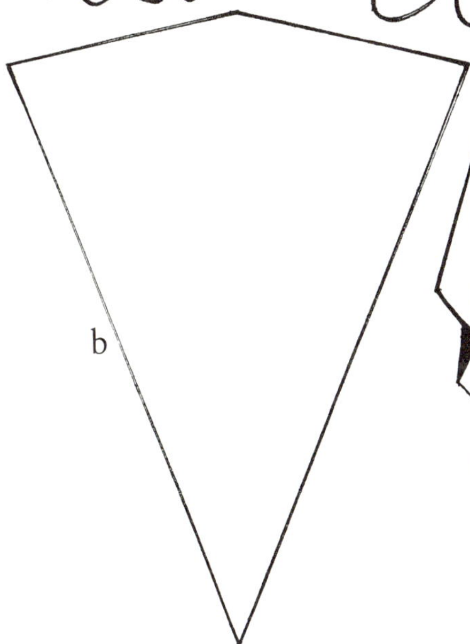

b

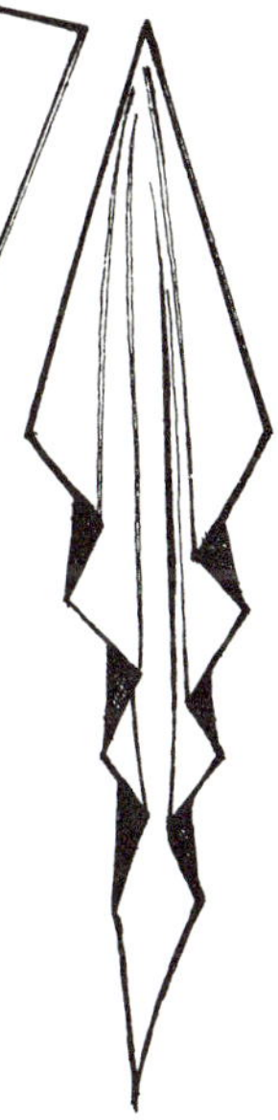

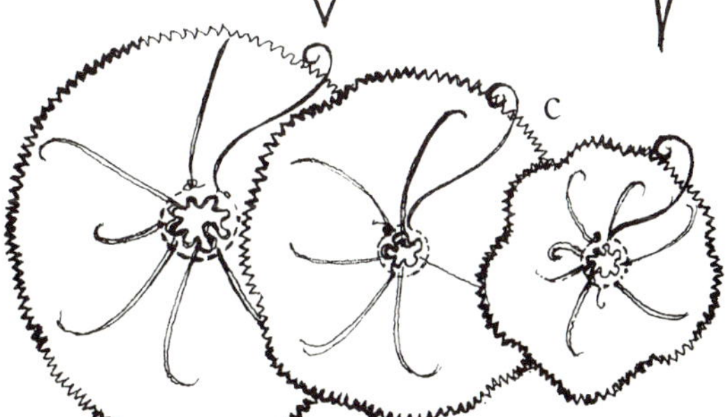

c

# Patchwork

Dior hit the fashion headlines with patchwork a little over a decade ago and the designers have been creating new versions for us ever since, opening our eyes to its ever-lively charm. Today we can see clothes that incorporate traditional patchwork designs in new ways and others that remind us but little of the intricacies of old.

Like crochet or knitting, patchwork can easily become a passion, and it has the advantage of being economical, relaxing and rewarding. The traditional art and technique consists of creating a design by assembling small shapes of differently coloured and patterned cotton or linen fabrics in an artistic arrangement. It is the skilful use of the basic shapes and colours which produces individual and creative results.

Whether you wish to make a bedspread, a border, collar and cuffs or a jacket, the basic method of patchwork is the same – that is, to join one piece to another edge to edge, or to apply pieces to a backing fabric in a decorative manner.

**How to start**
Buy a range of templates in plastic or thin metal or, if you prefer, make your own from scraps of cardboard. Make each shape of template in two sizes, the larger one for cutting out the fabric and the smaller for cutting out the paper shapes over which the patches are worked. Using the larger template, cut out several dozen pieces of differently coloured or patterned fabrics. Use the smaller template to cut out the same number of paper shapes. Place one paper shape on the back of each cut fabric shape, leaving an even seam allowance. Turn in the edges and tack them flat (b). Prepare a number of patches in this way, arrange them in a pattern and then stitch them together from the back (c).

**Random patchwork** (a)
Cut out large fabric shapes at random without templates or paper backings. Machine stitch them together with a zigzag stitch and cut away the seams to $\frac{1}{8}$ in. (3 mm).

A similar effect can be achieved by stitching patches on a contrasting background. Other variations include lapping, topstitching, padding individual patches, and joining sections together with fancy embroidery stitches such as coral, herringbone and feather stitches. Diagram (d) shows an example of lapped shell patchwork decorated with satin stitch motifs.

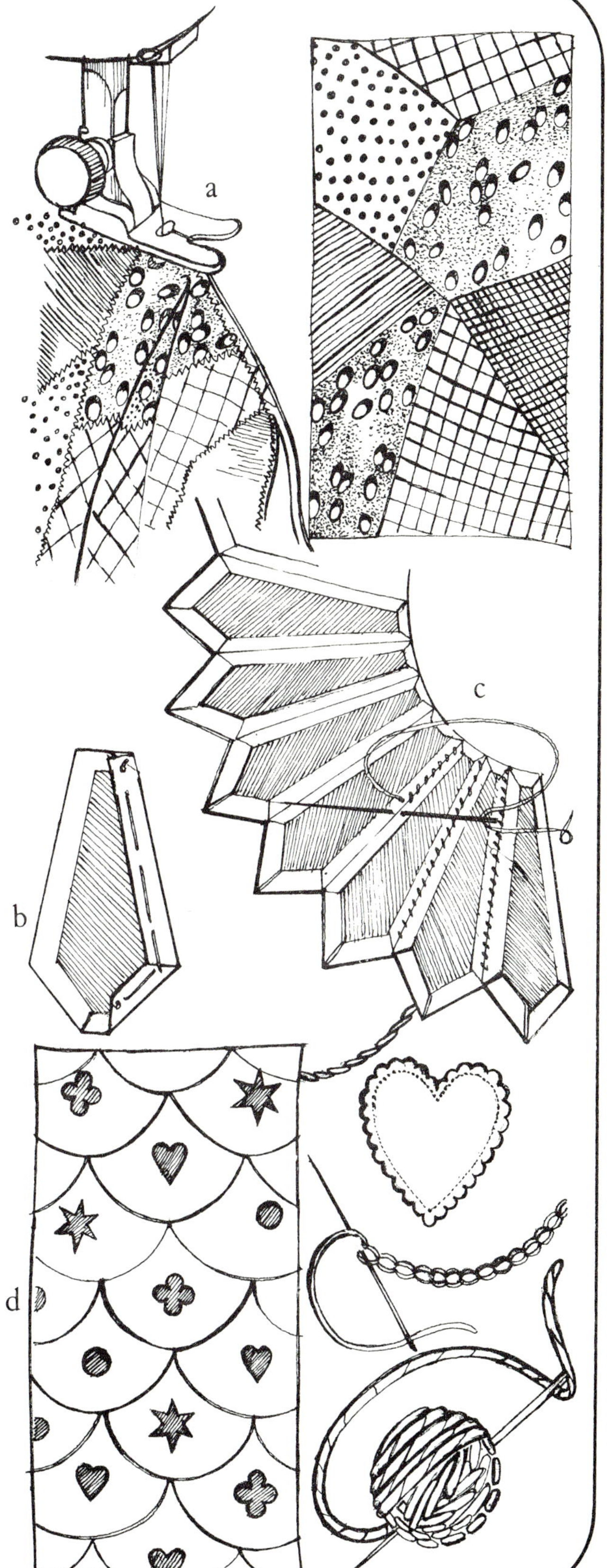

# *Knitting and crochet*

Instead of knitting a whole garment it is possible to work just one or two sections to combine with dressmaking. Because of its flexibility knitting is particularly suitable for midriff and body bands, wrist bands and yokes. Emphasize the originality of the idea by knitting matching headgear, scarves and hosiery and use the opportunity to invent striped and patterned knits, interesting colour mixtures and textured effects to incorporate as part of your design and complement your fabric. Crochet and knitting can be used to make trims and attractive edges for a multitude of garments as well as pockets, collars, belts, inset bands, purses, tasselled girdles and buttons. Crochet has the enormous advantage of being able to be worked directly on the fabric.

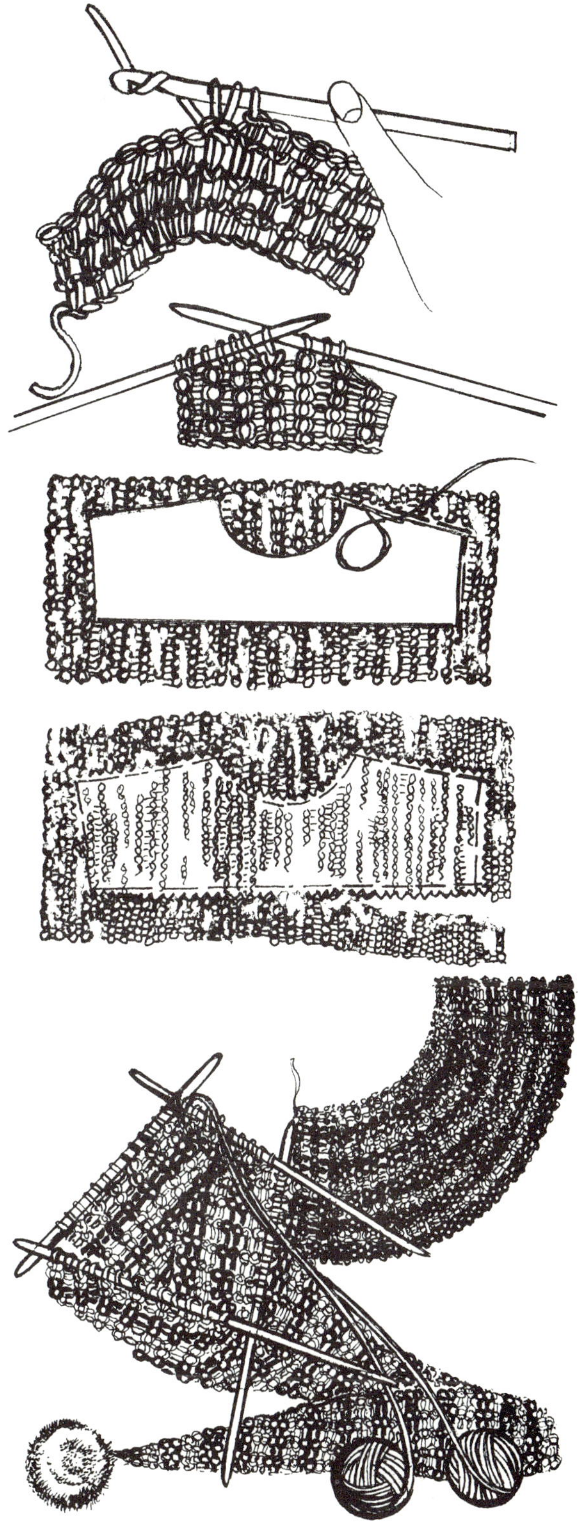

**Simple knitted sections**

Start by choosing a simple dress pattern, and select the pattern sections to be make in knitting – yoke, sleeves or bodice. Make a knitted rectangle larger than the pattern piece. Lay the paper pattern on the rectangle and tack along the stitching lines. Work in zigzag machine stitch $\frac{1}{8}$ in. (3 mm) outside the tacking lines and cut away the surplus knitting, leaving a normal seam allowance. The stitching will prevent the knitting from laddering and you can now use it as you would an ordinary piece of fabric. However, as knitted sections are more flexible than most fabrics, it is wise to tack the garment together to test for fit, allowing any small adjustments to be made before completion.

**More advanced techniques**

The experienced and adventurous will find it a simple matter to combine parts of a dress pattern with those of a knitted pattern. Try setting knitted sweater sleeves and turtle neck into a cloth tunic dress, a fully fashioned tight knitted body on to a gathered tweed skirt or a crocheted bodice into a simple dress. Choose yarns that match or contrast with the fabric and have fun with colours and textures.

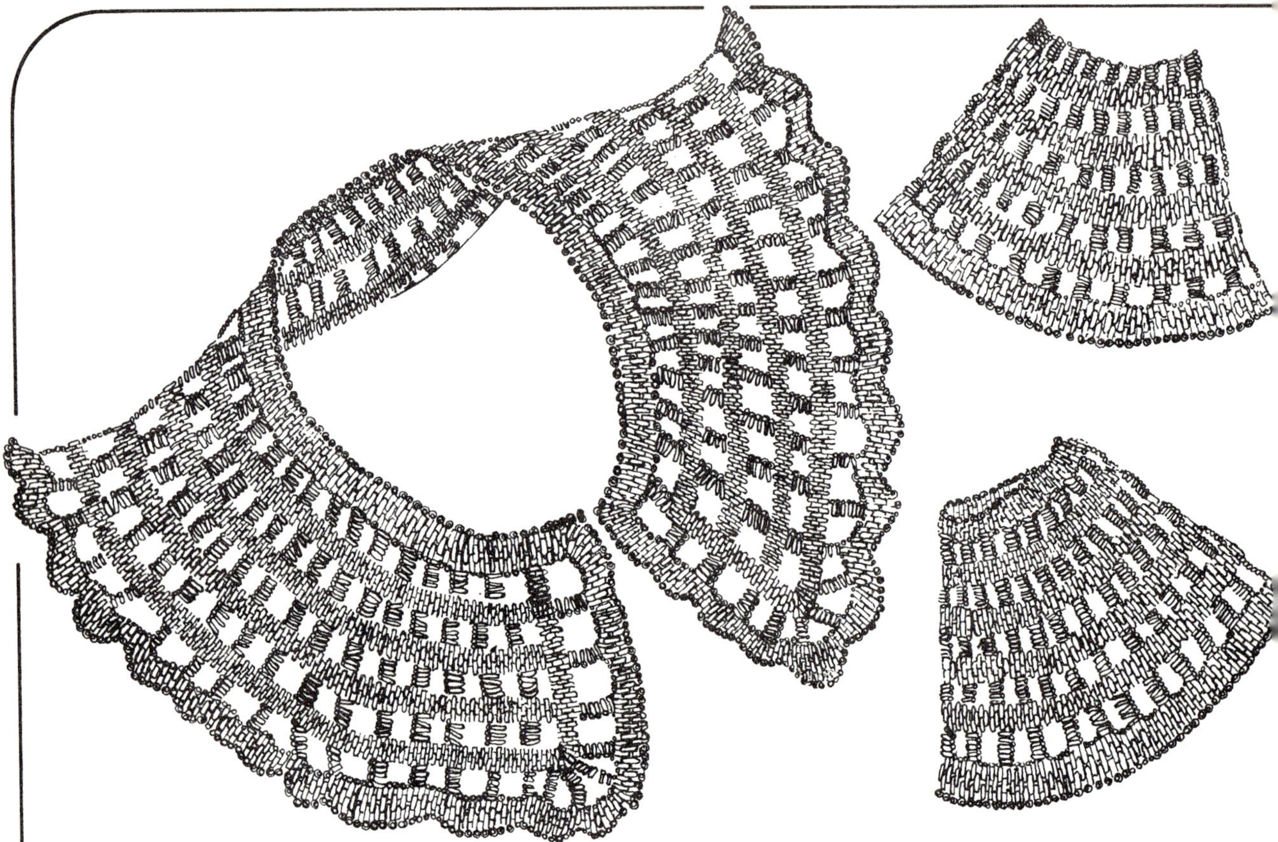

# *Crochet collar and cuffs*

Crochet continues to be a favourite for collars, cuffs and other dress accessories, perhaps because it takes little time and expense to achieve impressive results. Its charm lies in its simplicity.

This collar and cuff set is revived from the thirties. Crochet them in ecru or white cotton to wear on a plain dark dress or in gold or silver thread to make exciting evening accessories.

**Cuffs**

Using a fine crochet cotton and a 7 mm crochet hook, make 70 chain (a). Work three rows double crochet (c, d, e) picking up both threads of the preceding row. (See page 112 for U.S. crochet terms.)

*4th row* Crochet from left to right without turning the work. Make 10 ch., remove the hook and push it from front to back through 3rd d.c. of preceding row; pull 10th ch. through and slip stitch in position (b). Make 6 d.c. (c, d, e) on this chain, covering only 4 ch. *6 ch., slip end into 3rd d.c. of preceding row, 6 d.c. covering 4 chain*. Repeat from * to * to end of row. (This will leave 2 ch. free between each bar of d.c.)

*5th row* Without turning the work, crochet from right to left. *2 d.c. on the 2 ch., 1 d.c. on the d.c. bar*. Repeat from * to * to end of row.

*6th and 7th rows* Turn the work. Make 1 d.c. into each stitch.

*8th row* Without turning the work, make 11 ch., slip stitch end into 3rd d.c.; *6 d.c. over 4 ch., 7 ch., s.s. into 3rd d.c. of preceding row*.
Repeat from * to * to end of row, then 6 d.c. on final bar.
*9th row* As 5th row, but make 3 d.c. on chain loops.
*10th and 11th rows* As 6th row.
*12th row* As 4th row, starting with 12 ch. and using 8 thereafter.
*13th row* As 5th row, but making 4 d.c. on each chain loop.
*14th and 15th rows* As 6th row.
*16th row* As 4th row, starting with 13 ch. and using 9 thereafter.
*17th row* As 5th row, but making 5 d.c. on each chain loop.
*18th and 19th rows* As 6th row.
*20th row* As 4th row, starting with 14 ch. and using 10 thereafter.
*21st row* As 5th row, but making 6 d.c. on each chain loop.
*22nd row* Work down the side of the cuff again, making 6 d.c. on the chain and 2 d.c. on the rows of d.c.
*23rd and 24th rows* D.c. along three sides, making 5 d.c. into 1 d.c. at each corner. Finish off.
Press with a very damp cloth. Make a second identical cuff.

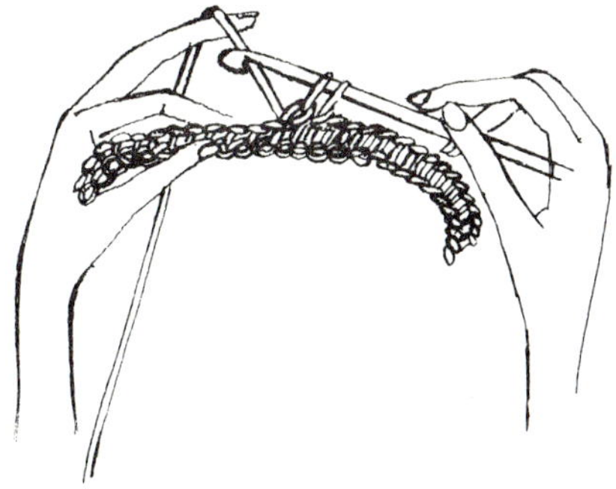

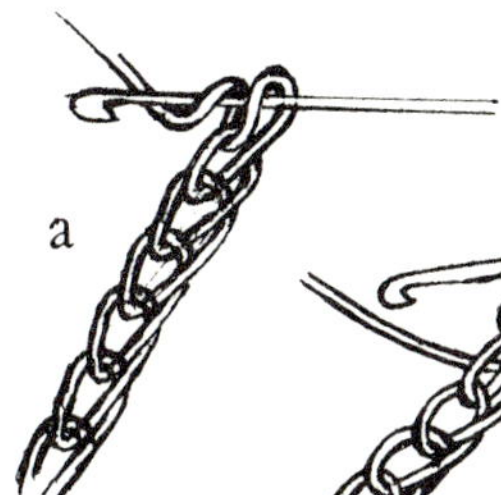

a

b

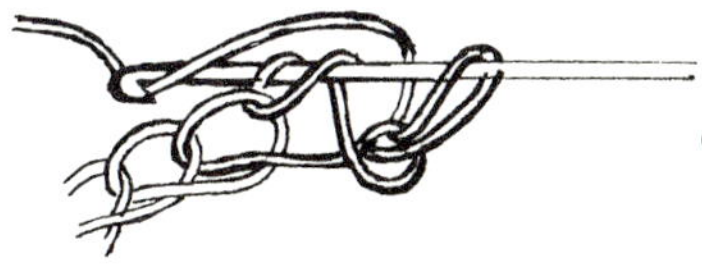

c

d

e

**Collar**
Work as for the cuffs, beginning at the neck edge. Make 150 ch. At the first row of loops, make 2 d.c. on each chain loop; at the second 3 d.c.; at the fourth 5 d.c.: then work all round the edge as for cuffs. Work one row of loops of 11 ch., then work back making 9 d.c. on each loop to make a wavy edge. Finish with 2 rows of d.c.

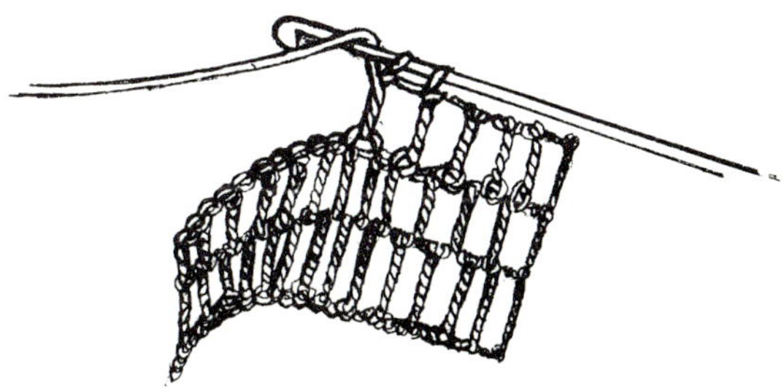

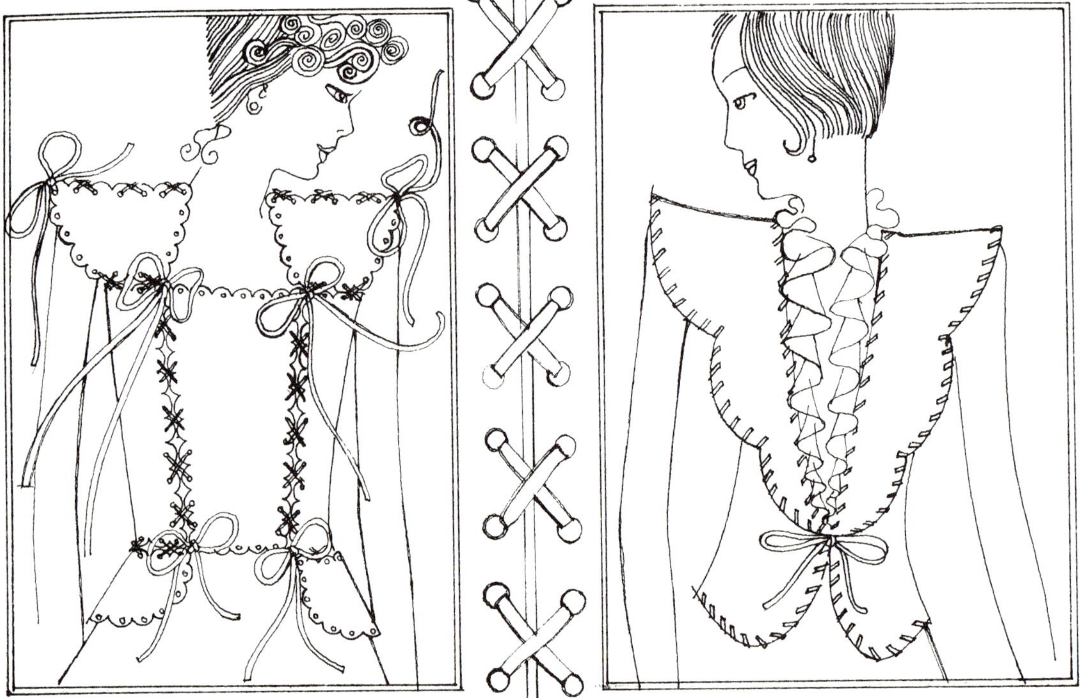

## *Easy ways with skins*

Fairly recent arrivals on the fashion scene are younger style model clothes made out of skins, soft suèdes and leather. New techniques in dyeing and production have brought a greater variety of skins on to the market, and many are even washable. Skins are non-frayable, and thus lend themselves to cutting without seams, using cut-edge treatments or simple overlapped seams. Decorative cut edges of all kinds can be used, of which pinking is the simplest, and exaggerated scallops and fake broderie Anglaise can also be made successfully. Suède strips threaded through punched holes will give a chunky look, lattice work of fine leather strips makes a very pretty surface, and a touch of punch-holing on cuffs, collars and pockets gives a sporting effect. For more fanciful decoration leaves and rosettes can be laid on the skin in relief, and elongated fronds of leather, each finished with a decorative end – a feather, a bead, a knot or a tassel – can make a garment look young and beautiful.

### Making up a garment

Remove the seam allowances from your paper pattern, adapting the seams and edge shapes to your own design. Try out the pattern on a dressmaker's dummy, mark any scalloped edges, and draw on the punch-hole positions. Lay the paper pattern on the wrong side of the skin and mark it out with a ballpoint pen. As the skin has no woven grain, the pattern sections can be placed at random, but you should avoid the underbelly and sections surrounding the limbs, which are of uneven texture. Cut out the sections accurately, using pinking shears or cutting scallop-fashion. Fix the sections together with Scotch tape or Sellotape and fit it on your dummy as for a normal garment, adjusting where necessary. Decide on the pattern of punching – straight, crosswise or diagonal – and punch the holes along the seam lines $\frac{1}{4}$ in. (6 mm) from the edge. The sections can then be thonged together using a blunt-ended thonging needle and thread, braid, thonging, fancy ribbon or string. Decorate the edges in a similar fashion and add decorative cut-outs as desired.

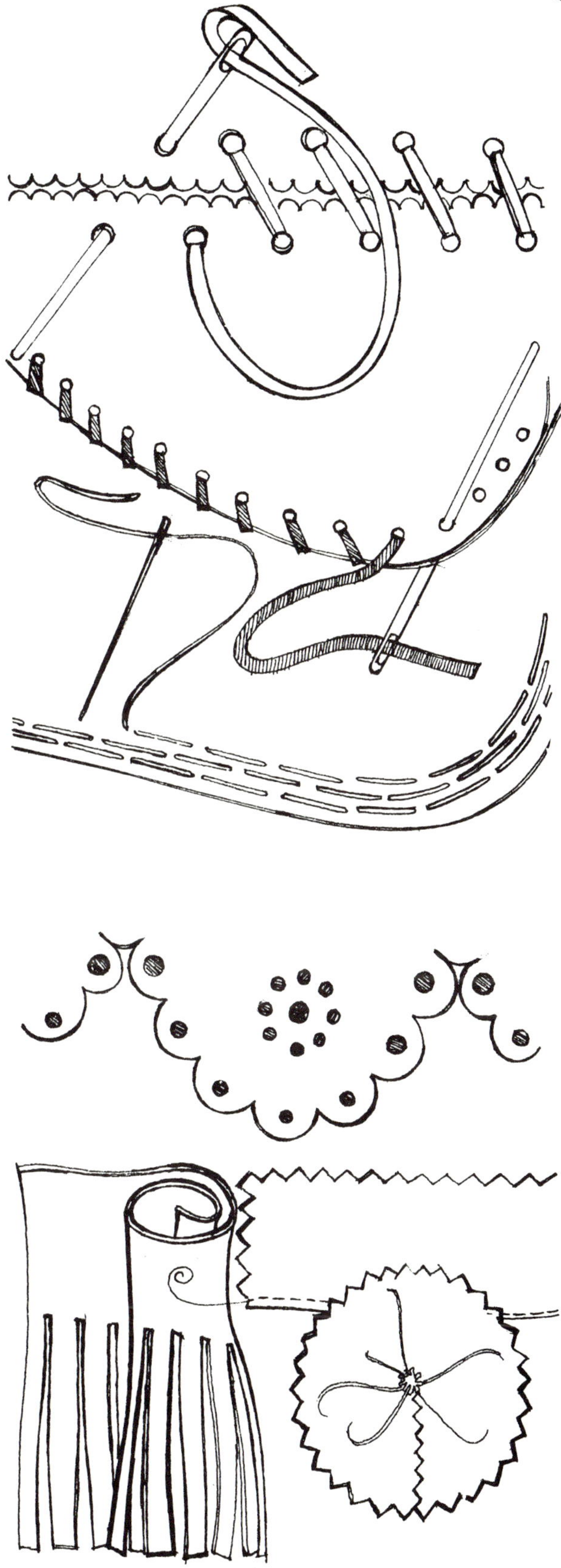

# *Furs – real, fun and fake*

When winter comes and snowflakes fall, when the thermometer drops to its lowest point, there is nothing like snuggling up into a piece of fur. Make a luxurious shawl collar in a long-haired fur, or let shaggy fox or Mongolian lamb peep out from round the edges of a coat. Snuggle your head into a hood lined with beaver, and warm your hands in an old-fashioned muff.

Choose from the wide selection of real and fake furs that are both cheap and easy to use. Look for rabbit, goat and lamb used as 'base' skins and cleverly converted into today's fun furs. Many are closely shorn, dyed and printed with patterns of ocelot, leopard, civet, giraffe or zebra – all useful for trimming small garments. Others are dyed mauve, blue or red to match up with plastics and high fashion fabrics.

**Fur collars and trims**

Remove the seam allowances from the paper pattern, and mark out the sections on the back of the skins or man-made fur, making sure that the pile always falls in the desired direction. (The pile should usually face downwards when the garment is worn.) Mark out the pattern sections with ballpoint pen, and cut them out from the reverse side with a sharp razor, using only sufficient pressure to cut through the skin and making sure that none of the pile is cut. If a small section has to be missed out in laying out the pattern, use overstitching to join on a piece of skin with matching pile (a). When the seam is opened out it will be concealed by the fur pile.

Use the same overstitching method to join the main sections of your garments. Finish the edges with tape. Pin the tape to the right side of the fur edge so that the fur protrudes a little. Oversew the tape to the edge (b), then fold it over on to the back of the skin and cross stitch it in position (c).

Use the same overstitching method make cuffs or trimmings for garments in fabric. Join them, right sides together, with zigzag machine stitch (d) or large cross stitch before proceeding as above.

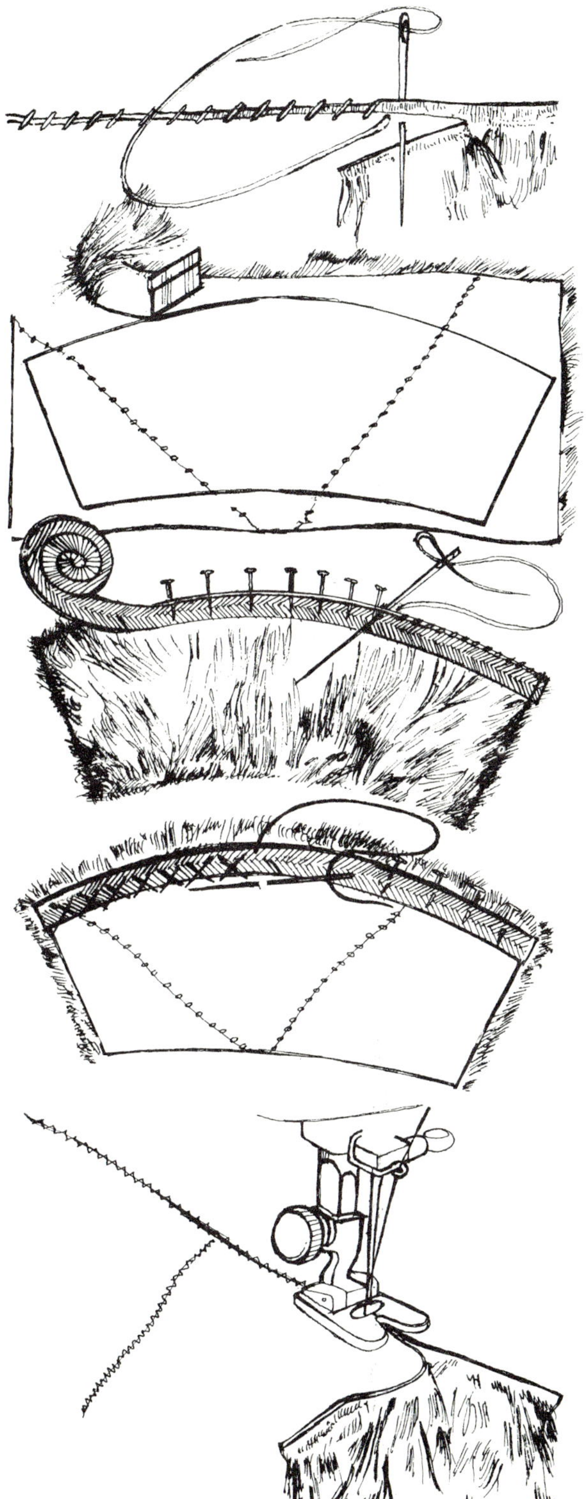

a

b

c

d

# *A flower for evening*

Why not make a single chrysanthemum in shadings of multicoloured organdie to trim your most glamorous dress, or a spray of two or three flowers to adorn a favourite hat?

**Making the petals**

To make the flower shown, you will need the following quantities of organdie: about one eighth of a yard (120 mm) each of pale pink, deep pink and mauve and slightly less than this of pale green, or the equivalent quantities in remnants. You will also need a small strip of covered wire for the stem.

Cut the pink and mauve organdie into strips $\frac{1}{8}$ in. (or 3 mm) wide. Now cut the strips into lengths as follows: ten 1 in. (25 mm) strips in deep pink for the centre; ten 2 in. (50 mm) strips in pale pink and ten in mauve for the next row; fifteen 3 in. (75 mm) strips in pale pink and fifteen in mauve for the outer petals. Shape one end of every petal to a rounded point.

Cut three leaf-shapes in green for each flower 2 × 1 in. (50 × 25 mm). Cut a piece of green fabric on the cross for the calyx 2 × 6 in. (50 × 150 mm) and a strip $\frac{3}{8}$ in. (or 10 mm) wide for the stems.

Now begin to roll the petal edges. Holding the fabric firmly between slightly moistened thumb and forefinger, turn the edges towards you and roll them between your thumb and forefinger until you have a neat curled edge all round. The tighter you twist the roll, the neater it will be. Roll the leaf edges in the same way.

**Assembling the flower**

Take about ten of the shortest, deep pink petals and sew them together to form a bunch. Now take bunches of five petals in the other colours and sew them round the centre bunch, the longer ones on the outside, rolled edges facing away from the centre. Arrange the petals loosely at the tips to give a realistic flower-like effect. Take a piece of wire 4 in. (100 mm) long and fix it firmly round the base of the petals. Fold the 2 in. (50 mm) strip of green organdie so that the short ends are together and wind it round the base of the petal to form a calyx. Sew it neatly into place adding green leaves at intervals, holding the ends in position with the green stem organdie binding. Bind the stem with the narrow green organdie. Finish by spraying lightly with a slightly sticky hair lacquer to hold it in shape.

**Other decorations**

You may like to make a boa, or a floating decoration for necks, hems or sleeves, or even as a hair ornament. Cut organza into strips of three different lengths – 9 in., 12 in., 15 in. (225 mm, 300 mm, 375 mm) – and cut the ends to form points. To obtain the curled effect, run each strip through your fingers over a pencil. This treatment will give a corkscrew look to the petals, which are then ready for use in any way you choose. Spray the finished boa with hair lacquer.

# *Ribbon flowers*

A popular pastime in the thirties was making garlands of ribbon flowers to decorate cushions and nightdress cases. Up-dated, they can make very pretty and unusual dress ornaments. They are easily and cheaply made from pieces of baby ribbon, and can be used to fill in any odd moments, rather like patchwork.

There is a surprising number of possible uses for ribbon flowers. Try mounting some on a narrow velvet ribbon to tie round your neck for an ultra-feminine neck ornament. Make a really gaudy garland of blues, scarlets and yellows interspersed here and there with an occasional deep shade of velvet to trim a summer dress or encircle the *décolletage* of a dark sweater. Spill a posy of flowers over a pocket, make a mock *boutonnière,* or scatter an entire dress or skirt with flowers like confetti.

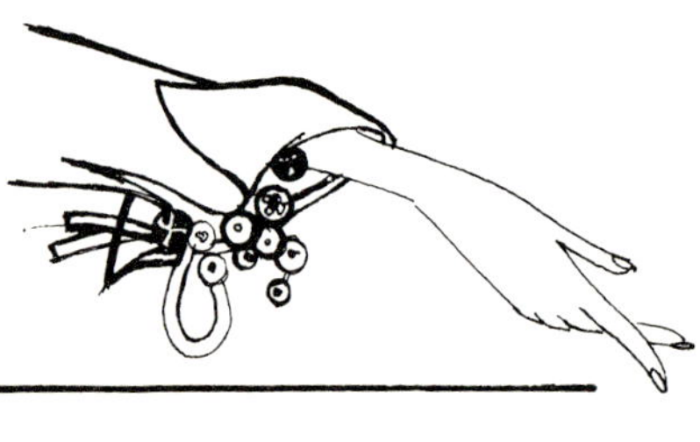

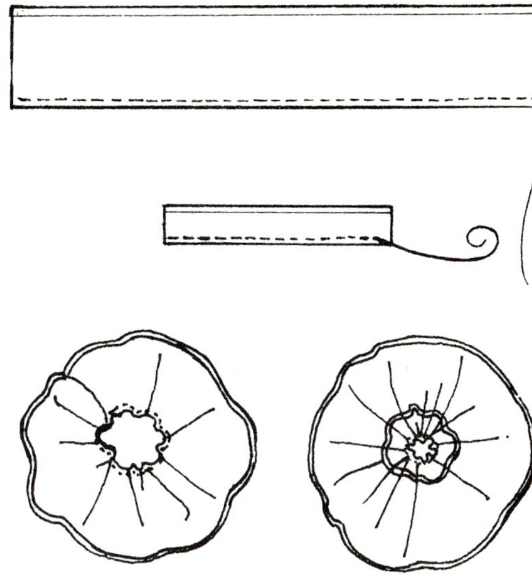

a

## Making simple flowers

Choose a mixed bunch of baby ribbons, using all the colours and textures you can find – satins, taffetas, velvets, moirés, grosgrain. For each flower you will need $\frac{3}{4}$ yd. (690 mm) of ribbon $\frac{3}{4}$ in. (20 mm) wide, and just under half that amount of $\frac{1}{4}$ in. (6 mm) ribbon for the centre. Gather each piece of ribbon separately along one edge, and draw them up into small circles (a).

Cut some green ribbon into 3 in. (75 mm) lengths and arrange them to make leaves (b). Group the flowers and leaves together and sew them firmly in place.

For a slightly bolder effect, combine ribbon flowers with couching (see page 16) and appliqué (page 54). Use a slightly wider ribbon, gathering the pieces as before, and sewing the flowers in position with French knots to represent stamens. Apply several flowers in the form of a garland with couched stems of rug wool or cord, and add leaves of pinked felt or leather.

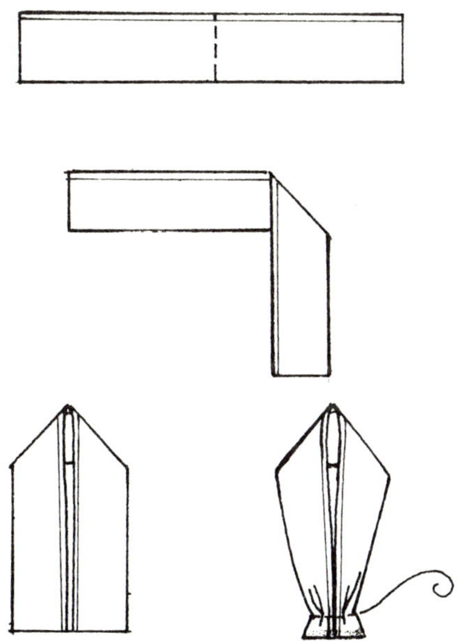

b

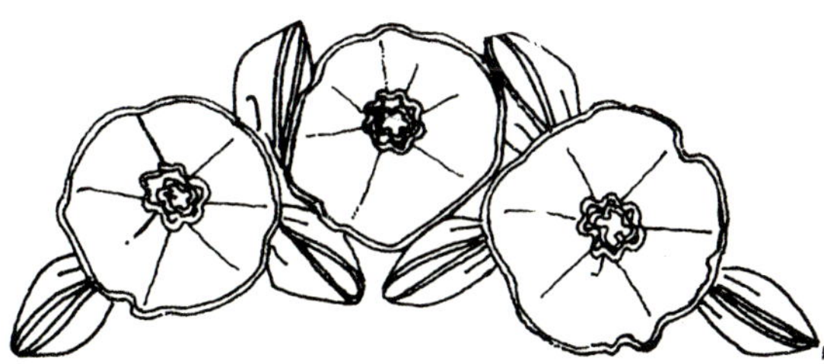

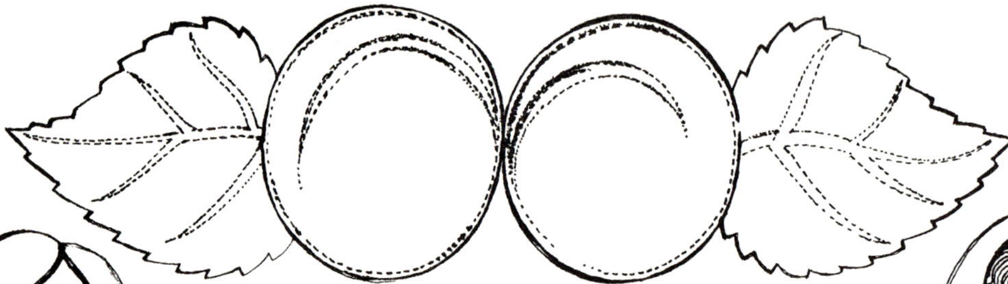

# *Fruit novelties*

Neither previous experience nor a standard pattern is necessary for making these fruit novelties. You will find quick ways around any problems and for inspiration all you need is a basket of real fruit to copy or interpret freely. Use your creations for all kinds of things – as decorative fastenings, for concealing ties or clasps, mounted on hairgrips, or dress pins.

Make the fruit in felt, choosing colours that most closely resemble those of natural fruit.

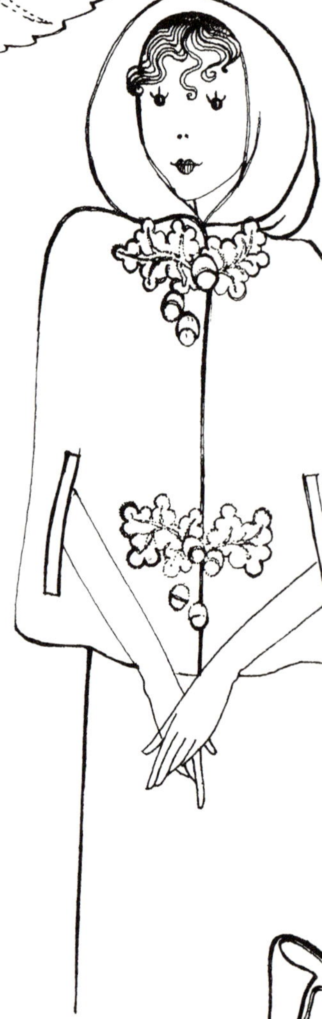

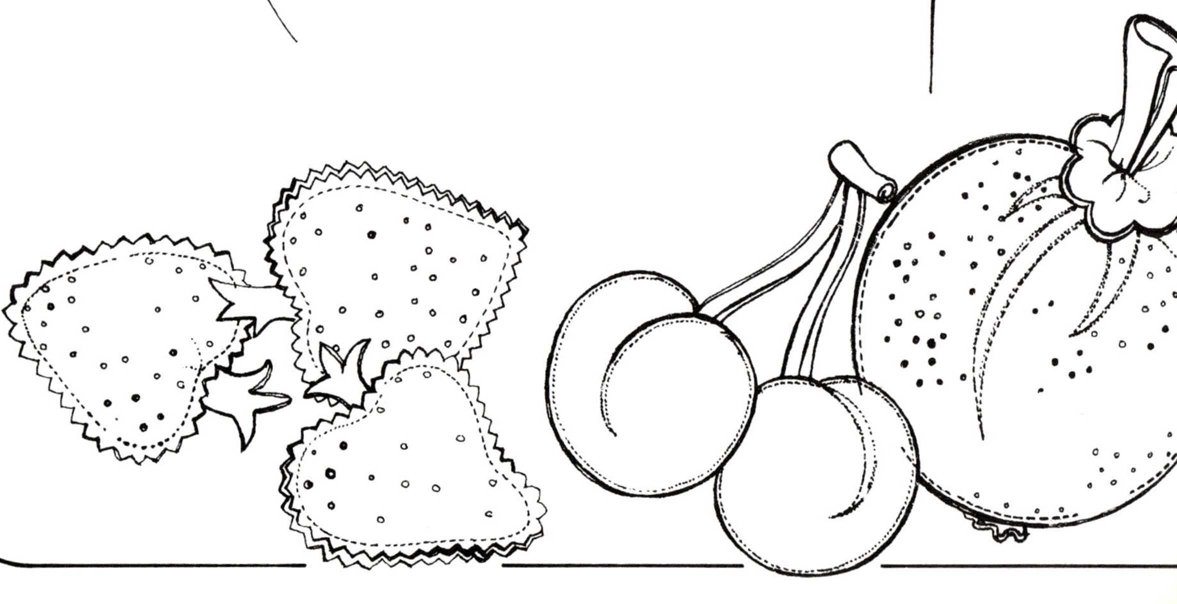

**Materials**
You will need a sewing machine, coloured felts, kapok or similar for the stuffing, fabric adhesive, a charcoal pencil, tailor's chalk, scissors and pinking shears.

**Strawberry**
Draw the shape on the felt fractionally larger than you want the finished fruit to be. Cut out two identical pieces, allowing $\frac{1}{2}$ in. (12 mm) seams and pin them together. Machine stitch round the shape, stuffing it softly as you go. Leave a small hole at the top centre, into which you will insert the stem.

Cut a felt shape for the stem (a) and curl it gently. Set it into the strawberry and machine stitch across the opening. Mark the seeds firmly with the charcoal pencil and finish by cutting round the seams with pinking shears (b).

**Oranges, cherries and plums**
Make these on almost the same principle as the strawberry. Mark and cut out the shapes and back each piece of the felt on to a light cotton cloth. Sandwich a layer of padding between the cotton and the felt. Draw on the indentation which appears in the fruit and stitch along it (c). Now continue as for the strawberry.

**Leaves**
Glue two, three or more layers of felt together one on top of the other, and draw a plain-edged leaf shape freely on the top layer. Mark the veinings with chalk and machine stitch over them several times to mark them distinctly before cutting a serrated outline (d).

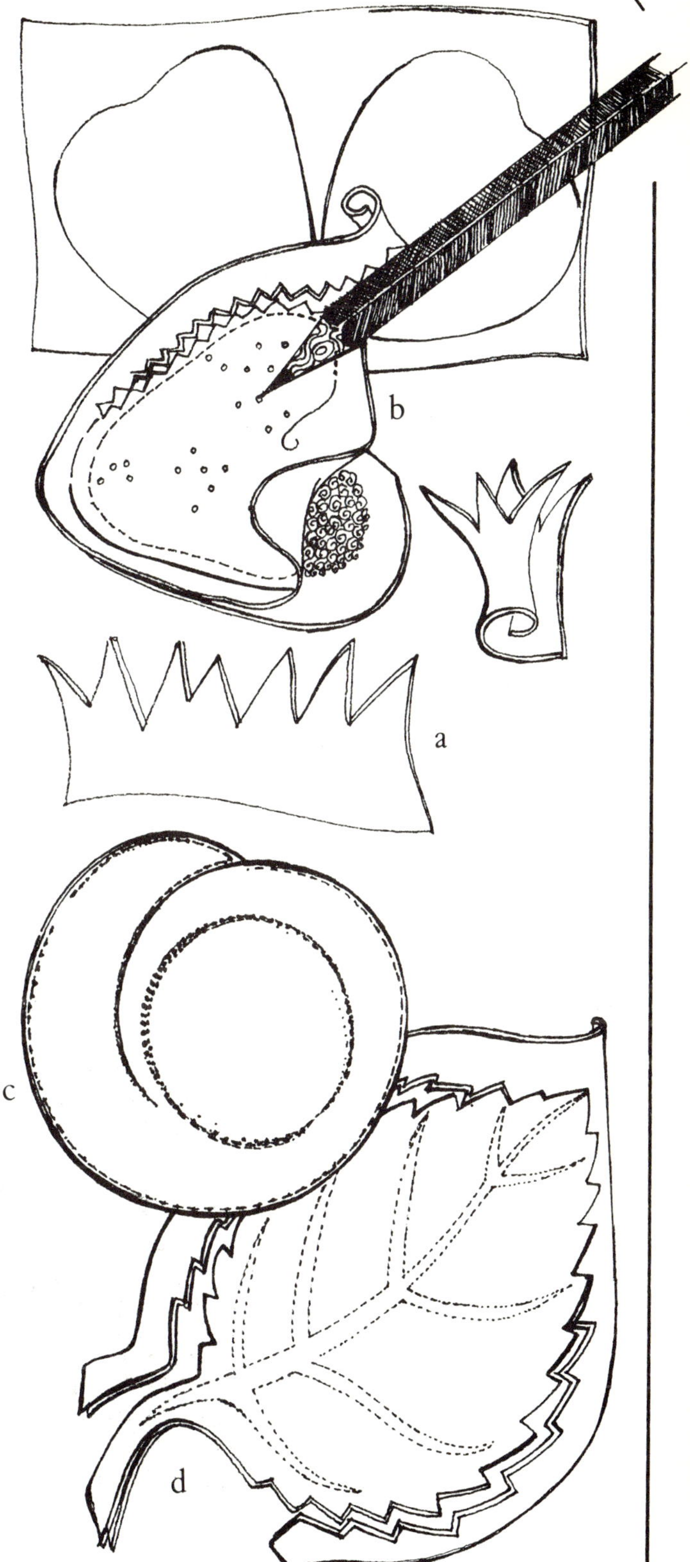

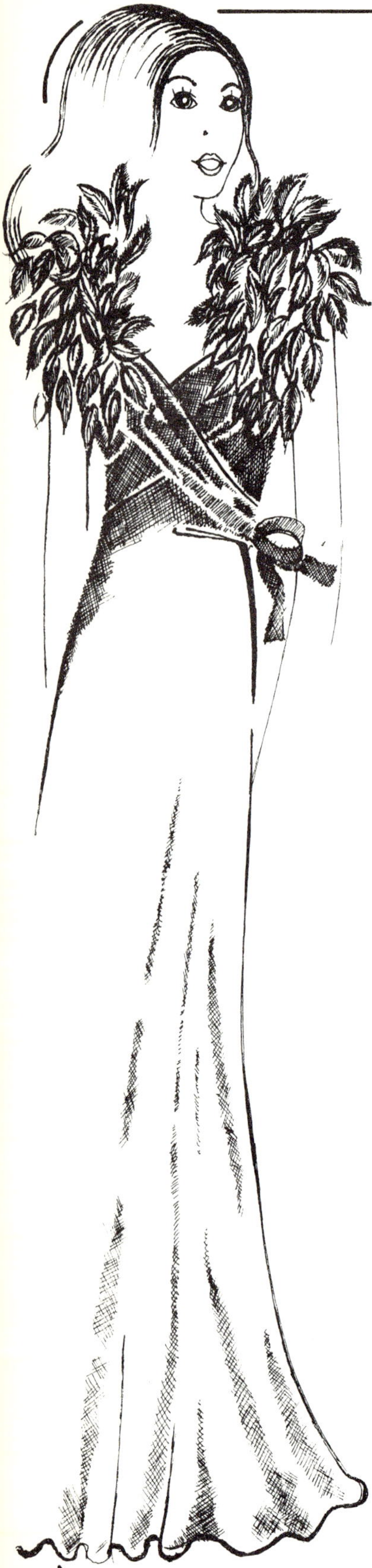

# *Feathers*

The natural vibrance of feathers cannot be manufactured. They feel good, look good, and complement both your complexion and the line and fabric of your clothes. Their allure has fascinated women for centuries.

Take a tip from pre-war Paris. Add style and femininity to the way you move and look by wearing feathers as a decoration on evening clothes or as a fashionable accessory. Imagine a long drifting chiffon scarf, its ends trimmed with ostrich; a ring of cock feathers round the neck of a sheer evening dress; a length of wide moiré ribbon decorated with feather flowers for head or neck wear, the long ribbon ends tied and dangling over the shoulder; a curved feather bracelet worn high on the arm; winter flowers to wear as a *boutonnière*.

The easiest feathers to obtain are those of the cock and the ostrich, dyed in an extensive range of colours. They may be bought by the yard or metre or, less commonly, in separate pads or plumes.

### Making a simple accessory

Buy a feather strip of your choice, and measure the exact amount required to make a loose neck or bracelet ring. Either stitch the ends firmly together or stitch on a hook and eye. For something a little more intricate, buy a length of wide ribbon, long enough to tie in a bow round your neck with flowing ends; then attach a feather strip to the central part, leaving the ends free. The stitching is worked firmly through the tape running through the centre of the feathers as for marabou (see page 36). For graded texture and colour effects, mix different strips of marabou, ostrich and cock.

### Stitching separate pads or plumes

Mount separate plumes on a narrow tape (b) to make a continuous strip. When using separate feathers to embellish a wide collar or scarf in crêpe or velvet, stitch each feather individually (a), whipping firmly over the stem and adding a dab of fabric adhesive for extra security.

### 'Winter flowers' as a flat decoration

Group five or six cock feathers together in a flower formation. Sew each one on separately with two or three side stitches, and fix a small bead at the heart of each flower.

### A boutonnière

Bunch five or six feathers together in upright fashion, glue the stems together, and wind thread around them. Finish by attaching 'stems' of bias tubing.

# *Tassels*

Tassels can be a charming form of decoration when used with flair and discrimination. Light and swingy, they will give a splash of colour and texture to any kind of dress.

Add tassels as finishing touches to girdles and points of hoods; dangle them pendant-style as necklaces; or sew them side by side in gay colours to make an attractive border fringe. Whatever the garment, there is sure to be a type of tassel just right for it. Design your own in varied lengths, yarns and thicknesses, with or without ornamental heads.

**A simple tassel**

Cut several pieces of thread or yarn twice as long as the tassel you need. Lay them

in a bundle and tie the centre tightly with a matching piece of thread. Fold the threads in half so that the ends match exactly and wind another piece of tassel thread tightly round them several times about $\frac{1}{2}$ in. (12 mm) from the top. Stitch the ends on to the tassel (a).

If you are cutting threads for several tassels, cut a strip of card the depth of one tassel and wind the thread round and round it. Cut along one edge to produce the correct thread lengths.

**Decorative tassels**
To make a tassel look full, knot a small bead to the centre strands underneath the head. For a large head, either make knots on top of one another in several of the outer strands or insert a shaped mould or bead into the bundle of threads when folding them in half and tying them down. Thread on another bead above the head to make a pendant tassel (b) or add beads of different shapes and sizes.

**Ornamental heads**
Cover moulds or beads with threads and band each section. Decorate the head with plaiting, a tube of crochet, basket-weave made of blocks of stitched yarns (c), lace stitch or embroidery.

**Beaded tassels**
These can be made in innumerable varieties by threading selections of beads on a strong thread, looping, twisting and knotting them together as you will. They can then be attached directly to the edge of the garment or suspended between other beads. Make a simple bead tassel by knotting beads on single strands of an ordinary tassel.

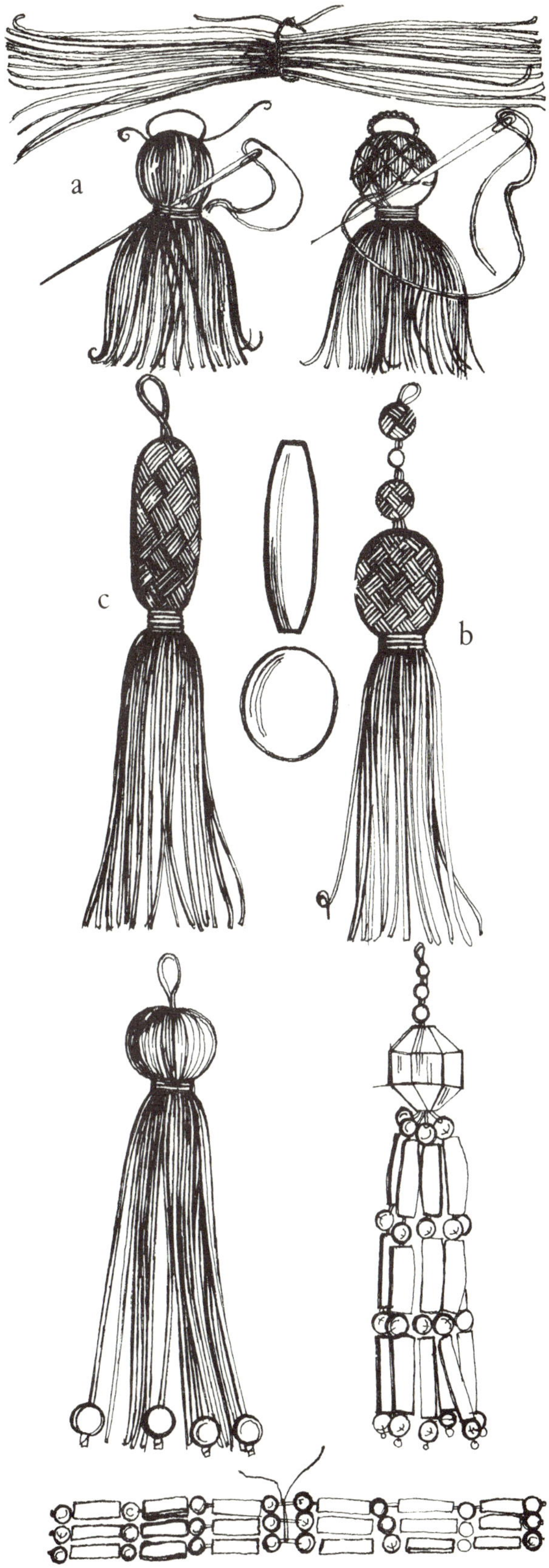

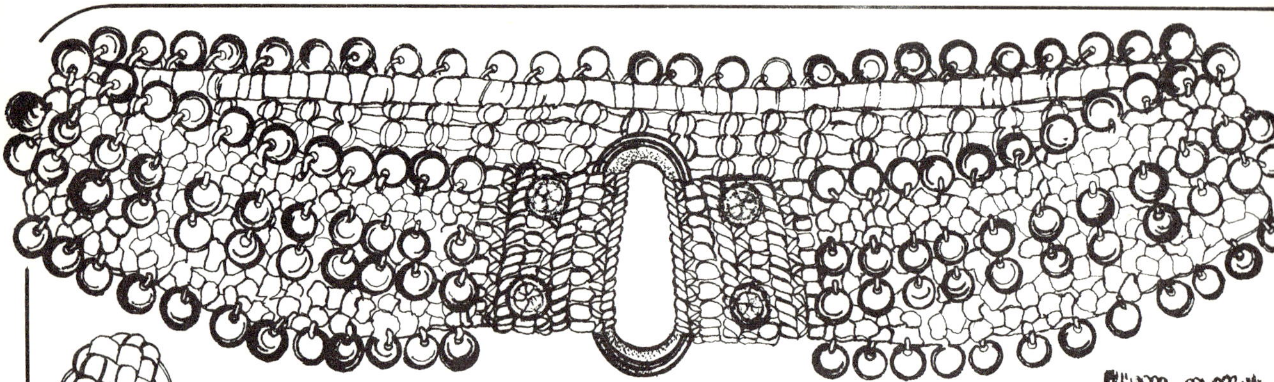

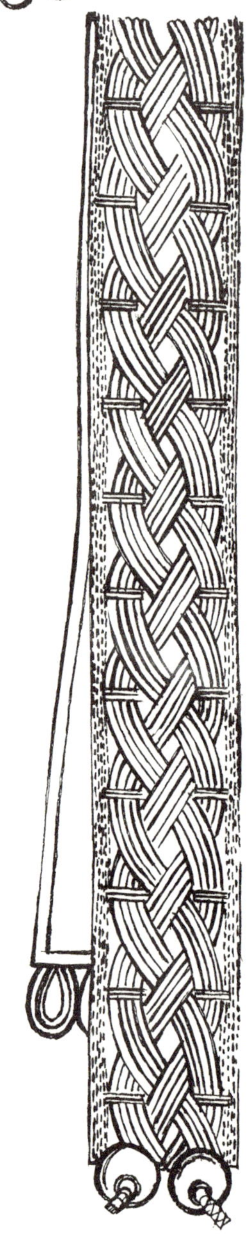

# *Yarn belts*

Yarn belts can be very desirable accessories. They are also fun to make in handworked crochet or plaiting, using crochet yarns, soutache or even parcel string.

**Crochet belt with beads**

Anyone familiar with simple forms of crochet will find this belt quick and easy to make. If you like to work to a pattern, cut one out in brown paper. Make it long enough to go round your waist, leaving ends for buttoning. Select thick, silk-type crochet yarn and a coarse hook, and thread gilded wooden beads on to the yarn before you begin. Crochet a length of chain to equal the width of the belt and continue in treble crochet. For this belt the ends are passed through a gilt buckle and buttoned down on either side, with buttons covered in matching silk.

**Webbing belt trimmed with plaited string**

You need a length of webbing your waist size plus 4 in. (100 mm) for seams, and a ball of parcel string. Turn under 2 in. (50 mm) at each end and stitch them flat. Cut eight lengths of string, each

measuring three times your waist size. Group these lengths into two sets of four, bend them in half and make a plait. Pin the webbing out on to a flat surface and spread the plait evenly along the face of the webbing, pinning as you go, leaving two loops at the beginning to act as fastenings. Stitch the loops firmly to the webbing. Knot two wooden beads to the ends of the plait to complete the fastenings. Fix the plait to the webbing with bars of couching in linen thread (see page 17). If there are coloured threads running through the selvedges of the webbing, match the colours of your bars to them instead.

**Plaited girdle of metallic soutache**
The girdle can be plaited to any length and finished with little rosettes or matching tassels (pages 32 and 104). If you prefer to have it as a belt, measure your work to meet exactly at the front of your waist and finish it with a pair of rosettes, one on each side, fixing a trouser hook behind them to clasp the belt together.

A simple plait needs six to nine strands of braid to look good, but can be rather wider. Try a length of plaiting so that you can gauge the finished width. Then, taking your findings into account, cut a paper pattern the exact width and length of the finished girdle. Mark on this the position of the blocks of plaiting and of basket-weaving. Pin the paper pattern out on a flat surface together with the strands of soutache, then plait and basket-weave the braid to the predetermined pattern. Secure the ends by winding them round with soutache to form a tassel.

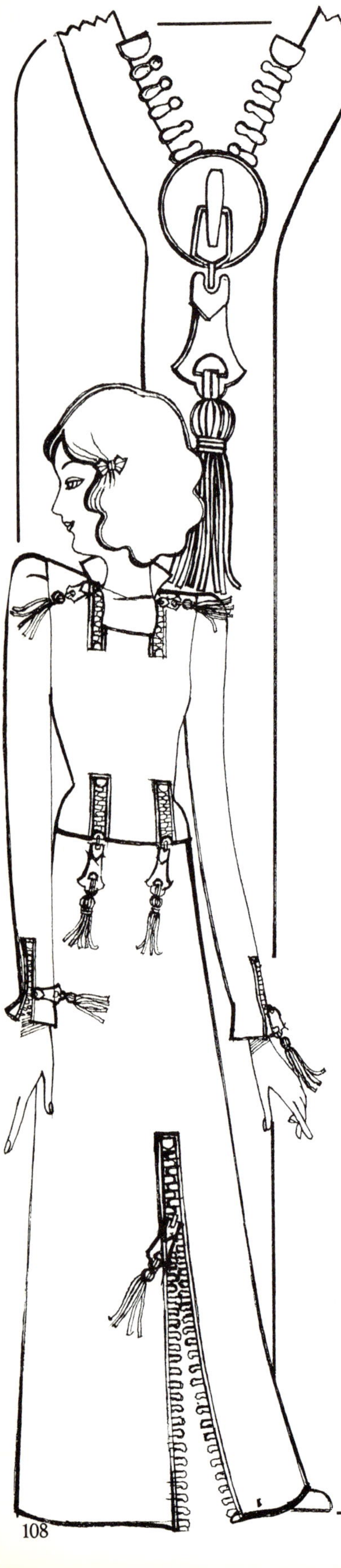

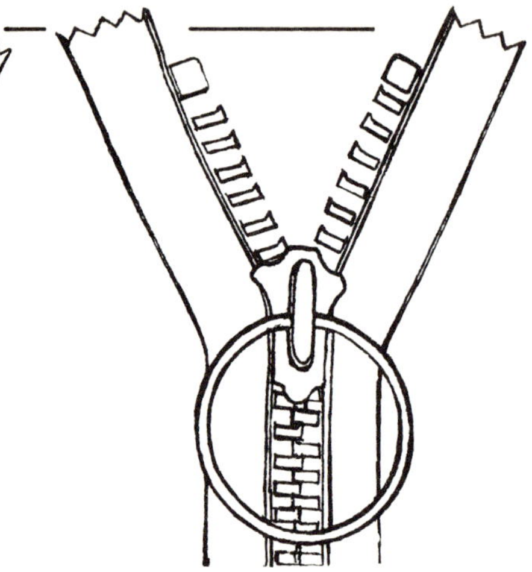

# *A bold zipper*

It was the 'bold zipper' with big teeth in metal, plastic or tortoiseshell, that made high fashion news for Schiaparelli, who exploited all things new. Today it is still the fastening with the most modern look. It no longer needs to be hidden from view, and designers have exploited it unashamedly as a fashion item in its own right. Zip up a skinny jacket for a streamlined look and set it off with zipped pockets to match. Zip and unzip a skirt half-way. And zip warm linings in and out of jackets. Flank your zippers with bold lines of topstitching, or with lines of contrasting piping, to make them even more prominent.

There is an enormous range of zip

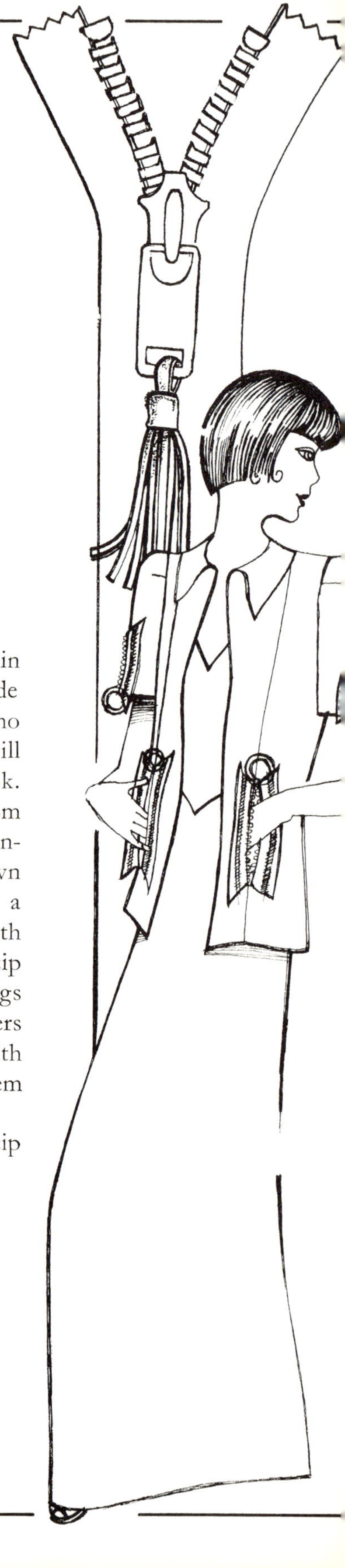

fasteners available. There are big bold ones in gay colours, with metal or plastic teeth, set on a variety of tapes which may be plain, contrasting or striped. Most dashing of all is the spiral zip, constructed with curved wires, and just right for accentuating a 'speedy' look. Some have bold rings and pulls or you can have fun trimming them yourself with tassels, motifs, beads and bobbles.

**Fitting a zip**

First mark the opening remembering that as your zip is going to show, you should allow a gap of at least $\frac{1}{2}$ in. (12 mm) between the long edges. Face the marked opening with matching thin fabric and tack the turned edges flat. Hold the zip in position with Sellotape or Scotch tape, secure it with tacking from the front and surface stitch it into position (a). If your zip is being let into a seam, clip the seam allowance to allow your seam to be opened at that important point. Stick the zip into position with Sellotape, secure it with tacking, and topstitch.

If the zip is to be let into the garment, rather than being used as a dress or skirt fastening, you will need to face the opening first. Cut a piece of matching lining fabric, lay it on the garment right sides together and tack it into position. Mark and stitch where the opening is to be. Cut along the middle and into the corners inside the stitching (b) and turn the facing to the inside. Tack it in place and proceed as before.

Decorate the pull with a tassel of fringed leather (c), embroidery yarns (see page 104), ribbons or any other fashion novelty that takes your fancy.

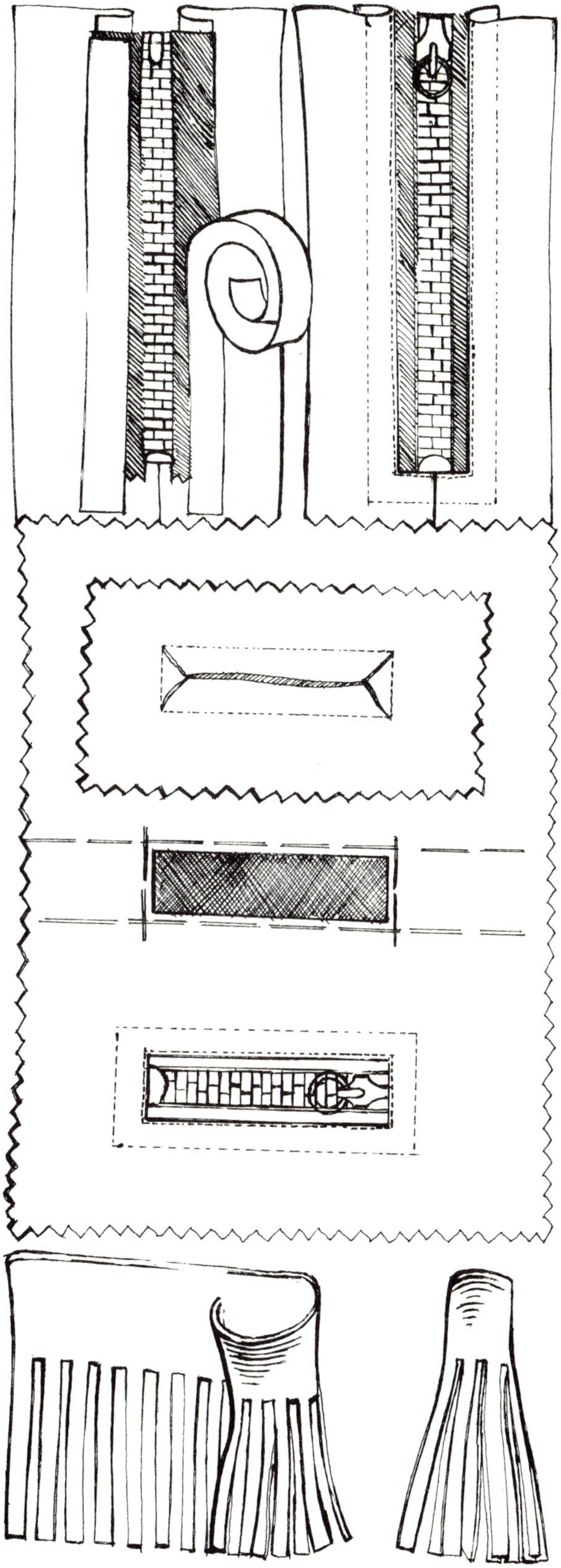

a

b

c

# *Frogging*

Frogging is easily adapted for all kinds of day and evening wear. Use it to fasten knitted cardigans, jackets, long coats, evening separates, caftans or tunics. Froggings, or Brandenburgs as they used to be called, were originally used as ornate fastenings on military uniforms. A single frog might spread across the entire width of a coat or jacket front.

Ready-made frogging is obtainable from major stores, but you may enjoy the freedom of designing your own. Make it in any weight of cord or braid – soutache, Russia, string or fancy flat braids. You can even use stiffened leather strips, crochet or rouleaux of matching or contrasting fabrics. Consider adding beads or sequins for evening clothes or team them with corded or braided buttons, with motifs, or with knots and *passementeries* (see page 58) on shoulder, yoke or pocket.

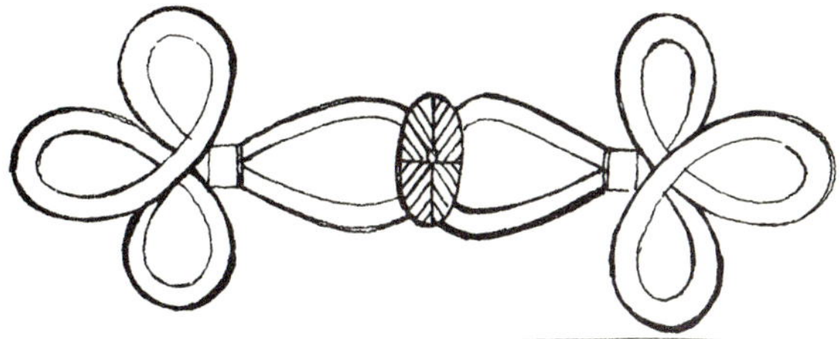

a

### Simple corded frogging

Draw the design on a strip of fairly stiff paper, experimenting with several versions before deciding which one suits the garment best. Lay the cord on one side of the design starting where the end can be hidden, and pin it into position as necessary (a). Stitch the cord overlaps together in such a way as to conceal the stitches, and finish the raw edges at the back. Repeat the design for the opposite side. If you wish, you may embellish the frogging with an extra loop or knot before sewing it on to the garment using a slip or stab stitch. Finish by selecting or making a button or toggle and stitching it into the left hand loop.

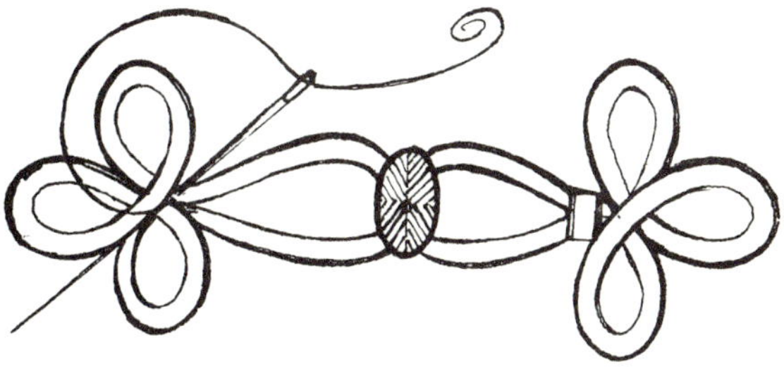

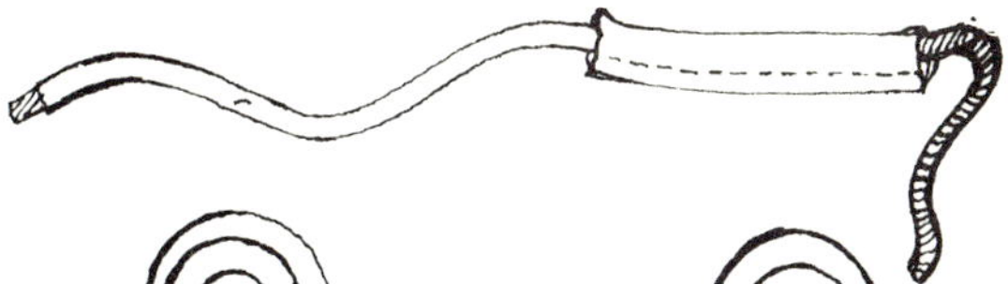

b

### Rouleaux frogging

If you would like to make a frog out of the same fabric as your garment or in a contrasting texture or colour, make corded rouleaux (b) as described on page 15. Twist and pin them into position as required. Side stitch curls or twists together from underneath (c).

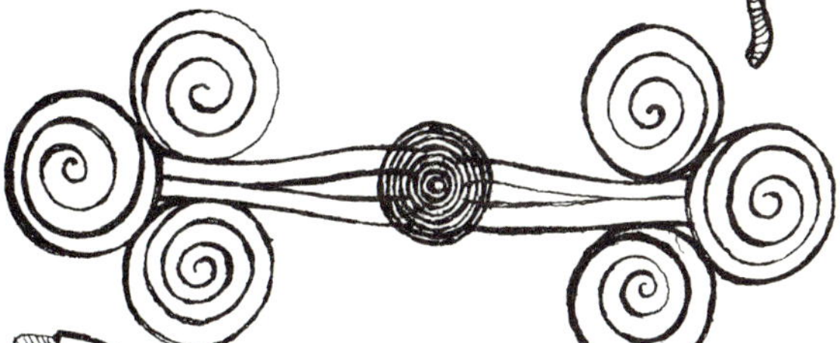

c

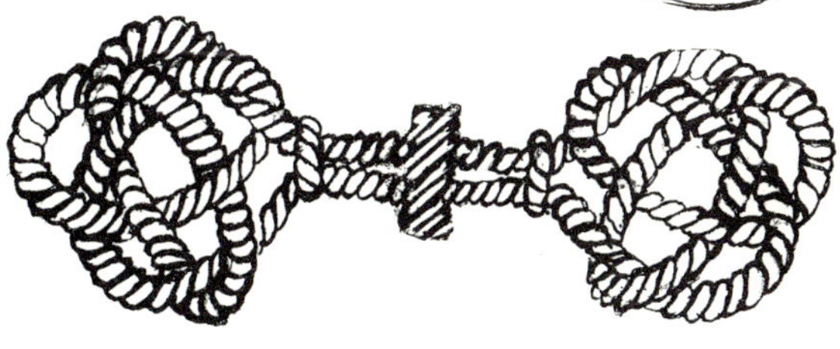

# *Glossary of fabrics*

**Angora** – Fine, fluffy, soft hair from the angora rabbit, usually mixed with wool or nylon. Cheaper imitations are made with common rabbit hair.
**Broderie Anglaise** – Embroidered cotton with lacy designs cut out of the cloth. Usually white, very feminine, popular as a trim or frill.
**Chenille** – Fancy material with a fuzzy appearance. Very popular in the fifties, and still used for dressing gowns and bedspreads. Made of cotton, viscose, or silk.
**Chiffon** – Light, delicate, sheer, open mesh. Made in silk and man-made fibres. Use french seams and rolled hems to prevent fraying.
**Crepe** – Light, plain weave fabric with a finely puckered surface created by chemically twisted yarns. Made in wool, cotton, silk and man-made fibres. **Moss crepe** has a characteristic, spongy texture. All crêpe fabrics hang and drape well.
**Crepe-back satin** – Or satin-back crêpe, has a satin face and a crêpe back, made in silk or man-made fibres.
**Crepe de Chine** – A slinky, raw silk fabric popular in the thirties, now also made in synthetic fibres. It has a finely crinkled surface and a soft, attractive gloss.
**Doeskin** – Soft leather made from the skin of a doe, also a closely woven thick black cloth with a smooth short nap, to resemble the original leather.
**Domette** – A plain cloth with a cotton warp and woollen weft used as an interlining.
**Ecru** – A term used to describe fabrics in their natural unbleached colour, a pale brownish beige.
**Faille** – Fine soft cloth originally made of silk, with a slight cross rib.
**Gauze** – First made in Gaza, a lightweight, thin, open textured fabric rather like cheesecloth, made of natural cotton, used for bandages. Filmy, silk gauze (**Lisse**) and linen gauze are also available.
**Georgette** – Heavier than chiffon, a fine, sheer, light fabric, with a crêpe texture, made of wool, silk or man-made fibres.
**Grosgrain** – Has a pronounced, but fine, one way horizontal rib, and is made from silk or man-made fibres. Used for dresses and to make ribbon.
**Lame** – Glamourous evening fabric into which metallic threads, usually gold or silver, have been woven.
**Lawn** – A kind of fine linen, resembling cambric, used for Bishops' sleeves, and light summer clothing. It sometimes has a satin weave stripe, and can also be made of cotton or cotton synthetic mix.
**Leno** – A kind of cotton gauze, used for caps, veils and curtains.
**Matelasse** – A multi-weave with a quilted appearance, sometimes combined with metallic threads. Originally a French dress goods of silk, or silk and wool, having a raised design.
**Mohair** – Long, silky, light hair from the Angora goat, woven into fabrics used for coats, suits and knitwear.
**Moire** – A finishing process which can be applied to silks, cottons and man-made fibres, giving a watered, variegated appearance to the surface.
**Mull** – Very fine soft cotton fabric with an open texture, used for dresses, veils and turbans, and for lining lightweight materials.
**Muslin** – Usually made of cotton, but can be of silk or worsted. A pretty, delicate, woven fabric, used for children's and ladies' dresses, it can be stiffened for lining, or for caps and collars, and a heavier version is used for shirts.
**Organdie** – Plain weave cotton fabric, fine and transparent, with a translucent look and a permanently stiff finish. Used for frills, stiffenings and dresses.
**Organza** – A fine transparent fabric similar to organdie. Originally made of silk, imitations are now made with synthetic yarns. **Satin organza**, made with a satin weave, has a shiny face and crêpy back.
**Sheers** – A term used to describe light filmy fabrics such as georgette and organza.
**Silk** – The fibres are taken from the cocoon of the silkworm. Strong, soft, lustrous thread is spun from the filaments, and woven into fabric. Silk fabrics are made in many different weights and weaves, including damasks and brocades. Waste silk from defective cocoons and short lengths of filament are spun like cotton to make spun silk. **China silk** is a flimsy lightweight silk cloth used for lining. **Habutai** is Japanese silk, soft and light, but heavier than China silk. **Pongee** was originally a handwoven, light, wild silk made in China. Imitations are now widely made in man-made fibre or mercerized cotton. **Raw silk** is a fibre which is coarser than ordinary silk, made by reeling together the filaments from several cocoons before the natural gum has been removed. **Wild silk** and **Tussah** are fibres from wild silk worms who eat other foods than mulberry leaves. They are made into **Tussore** and **Shantung**, which are darker and stronger than cultivated silk. Shantung has a rough irregular quality. **Thai silk** is a plain weave silk made in Thailand, often in large plaid designs with brilliant, exotic colours. **Art silk** was the first cheap, artificial silk, and was popular for lingerie in the thirties. Silk can be shot (*see* taffeta).
**Taffeta** – A close weave, crisp material with a faint rib, originally made of silk. Cheaper versions made of man-made fibres are now commonly used for lining material. Shot or shaded taffeta is woven with contrasting colours so that the fabric appears different colours when viewed from different angles. **Paper taffeta** is a thin crisp taffeta which was very popular in Victorian times.
**Tarlatan** – A kind of thin, open muslin, used for ball-dresses.
**Tulle** – Fine, machine-made net, of silk or man-made fibre, used for veiling and ballet dresses.
**Tweed** – Rough-surfaced twill weave wool fabric. Two or more colours are usually combined in the yarn to give a rich, flecked colour mixture.
**Veiling** – Very fine, light fabric usually made in quality yarns like silk or worsted. Used for nuns' veils, millinery and children's clothes.
**Voile** – Light, crisp, open textured fabric, of wool, cotton or man-made fibre. Used for dresses and blouses.

### Crochet Stitch Terms

| BRITISH | AMERICAN |
|---|---|
| single crochet | slip stitch |
| double crochet | single crochet |
| half-treble crochet | half-double crochet |
| treble crochet | double crochet |
| double-treble crochet | triple crochet |
| triple-treble crochet | double-triple crochet |
| quadruple-treble crochet | triple-triple crochet |
| long treble | long triple |